THE TASTE OF
THAILAND
VATCHARIN BHUMICHITR

สวัสดี.

คุณแม่ที่ความรัก.

For my mother

THE TASTE OF
THAILAND
VATCHARIN BHUMICHITR

Food photography by Clive Streeter

Specially commissioned location photography
by Michael Freeman

PAVILION

This edition published in Great Britain in 1991 by
PAVILION BOOKS LIMITED
196 Shaftesbury Avenue, London WC2H 8JL

First published in 1988

Text copyright © Vatcharin Bhumichitr 1988
Recipe photographs (by Clive Streeter)
copyright © Pavilion Books Ltd 1988
Line illustrations (by Jane Evans)
copyright © Pavilion Books Ltd 1988
Location photographs copyright © Michael Freeman 1988
For other photographic acknowledgements
see page 220

Designed by Andrew Barron Associates

British Cataloguing in Publication Data
Bhumichitr, Vatcharin
    The taste of Thailand.
    1. Cookery, Thai
    I. Title
    641'.59593   TX724.5.T5

ISBN 1 85145 183 8 (hbk)
ISBN 1 85145 703 8 (pbk)

10 9 8 7 6 5 4 3 2 1

Printed and bound in Singapore
by Toppan Printing Company

*Photograph on pages 2/3: Detail from the entrance doors
of the Temple Wat Phra That Haripunchai
page 6: Chiang Mai at dawn, mist from the northern
mountains*

CONTENTS

*Khao Sam Lawy
Yod National Park,
Southern Thailand*

INTRODUCTION

*Previous pages:
Scenes from town
life in old Siam:
making music,
offering food,
chewing betel nut.
A mural in Wat
Mongkut, Bangkok*

The taste of Thai cooking is easy to identify: lemon grass and fish sauce, coriander, galangal, garlic, sweet basil and coconut milk all combine to make a harmony that is unforgettable. As is the look of the food: set out in a group of small dishes on which the ingredients have been decoratively arranged, with vegetables carved as flowers, fish and meat arranged in neat patterns, tiny bowls of clear soup steaming beside a communal pot of fluffy rice. Surprisingly, it has taken a long time for Thai cuisine to reach the West but now it has, the growth in its popularity seems unstoppable, with restaurants opening in the major cities of Europe and America almost daily. Partially it is Thailand's geographical location, reflected in its food, at a point half way between India and China that must appeal to the Western palate. But it is also the lightness of the food and the way it corresponds to recent nutritional thinking that has made it so popular: meat, always without fat, makes up only a small proportion of a Thai meal, the largest element being quickly cooked vegetables that remain firm with all their flavours preserved. Thai food is seldom cooked for long and is always fresh.

Every Thai is interested in food. Because we believe that life should be *Sanuk* or fun, the pleasures of eating are very important to us. Preparing food well and serving it beautifully is never a chore, perhaps because much of Thai cooking is very straightforward. Few dishes take longer than eight to twelve minutes to cook. A Thai meal allows the chef considerable style without having to disappear into a kitchen all evening – we love to have guests in Thailand but we like to be with them, not somewhere out of sight.

The good news for those wishing to make our food is that even the more sophisticated dishes photographed in this book will not involve an arduous programme of cordon-bleu-style cookery lessons. This book has been carefully graded so that you can begin with one or two elementary dishes yet soon be able to set out a full Thai meal with all its unique flavours. The other good news is that you need buy only a few special ingredients in order to start at once: the average modern cook has most of the basics to hand as well as the equipment needed so this will not be a costly exercise. Happily, Thai cooking is about flavours and methods, and not about rituals, and these methods can be applied to whatever ingredients are available locally. Our country is often called the crossroads of Asia, and we are very open to outside influences and love to experiment, so if you cannot get oriental vegetables then use whatever seems the nearest local equivalent, any Thai cook would do the same quite happily.

It is the range and adaptability of Thai cooking that raises it beyond the level of just another local cuisine. All occasions, private and public, all ceremonies, all the important moments in our lives have food somewhere at the heart of them. Offering food to a monk in his saffron robes during the morning alms gathering makes food an essential component of our religious faith. Visitors are often amazed at the lengths we go to in our search for the unusual – on the outskirts of the city of Korat is an unattractive concrete building which appears to be mainly a garage during the day, but at night it is a restaurant whose speciality is the most wonderful duck. Scruffy it may be, but rich businessmen and well-dressed women are not averse to putting up with its drawbacks for the pleasure of its food.

One word of warning, Thai food is addictive, you may not want to eat Thai food every day but you will certainly want to return to it often. When I first came to London as a student in 1976 this was a problem as it was virtually impossible to find even those few essential ingredients that give Thai food its special character. There were four Thai restaurants in London struggling to serve a facsimile of our cuisine, but even so it was easier to give up the idea of eating Thai and settle for a Chinese

Village at early morning. The traditional offering of food to passing monks

meal. Of course we went on trying to conjure up echoes of home in our flats and bedsits and the arrival of a visitor from Bangkok with a fresh supply of raw materials would be the excuse for a party. It was a visit to my brother in Chicago that showed me a different lifestyle, for there, as in New York and Los Angeles, a large Thai community had led to the setting up not only authentic restaurants but also of supermarkets with everything a Thai cook needs. While I was still a student the great surge in tourism to the Far East brought with it a wide public keen to find again the food they had enjoyed on holiday. It began to look as if that American experience could be repeated in London.

Part of my family are hotel owners and restaurateurs and I had worked with them before I left for England. They agreed that I should test my theory and when my studies were over I opened a shop selling Thai produce. The results were electric, not only did addicts both Thai and British flock to buy the sauces and fresh vegetables flown in every week, but suddenly rivals were springing up all around. Enough of shops I thought, it's time to really produce the food and so I opened the Chiang Mai restaurant in Soho determined to be among the first to prove that Thai food outside Thailand could be absolutely authentic. I began by doing much of the cooking myself and have gradually trained a band of helpers with myself on hand to ensure that there are no lazy concessions to some mythical notion of Western taste. I'm happy to say that for some time now the restaurant has been the only Thai establishment in the *Michelin Guide,* and the *Good Food Guide* has said that the Chiang Mai is among those responsible for the renaissance of Soho as a culinary centre. This book is a response to the requests of those who regularly come to the Chiang Mai and ask me to recommend a practical guide to cooking Thai meals at home. Because of the intimate relationship between Thai life and the way we eat, each chapter takes a look at an aspect of the country and the food that comes from it so that the meals you are making will have a context. There is food that a rice farmer or fisherman might enjoy and there's special food for great festivals and royal occasions. I have tried to create a portrait of a people who consider their cuisine to be an art, a ceremony, an offering.

To help ensure that everything works, I enlisted the support of a friend, Jackie Hunt, who undertook to learn from scratch how Thai cuisine operates. Jackie's mother was a professional cook and Jackie first encountered Thai food in America where she lived for seven years, so she has been also able to translate my recipes for the American kitchen. Jackie has watched me cook all the dishes here, has noted everything down then gone off to try for herself. We have eaten a great deal of Thai food over the past year!

So please give it a try. We start with the equipment and ingredients you'll need along with some advice on techniques, but from then on it's a steady progression of dishes, from elementary to fairly complex; just go as far as you wish. We Thais are very individualistic and easy-going in our cooking and when you have learned the basic rules you can vary the taste to suit your own palate, a little sweeter or a little more savoury, hotter or milder, it is up to you. My hope is that with the aid of my book you will find that your meals are a little more *Sanuk*.

Dusk. Thara, near Krabi, Southern Thailand

FROM SIAM
TO THAILAND

A BRIEF HISTORY

A colossal statue of the Buddha smiles serenely from the shadows of a ruined temple, its walls overhung with tropical vegetation. There is an echo of clicking cameras and a party of tourists shuffles back onto their coach. In under an hour they will have been whisked in air-conditioned luxury from this image of ageless beauty to the honking nightmare of Bangkok's rush-hour traffic. When they return home they will take away a jumble of memories: straw-hatted peasants bending to tend their rice in a flooded paddy, soaring sky-scraper banks, a fairy-tale royal palace with gilded roofs, bustling markets where they were offered anything from grilled squid to an imitation Gucci bag. Before they came they probably had nothing more than a few misconceptions gleaned from Yul Brynner in *The King and I*; but when they leave they will have experienced contradictions so strong few can begin to reconcile them.

Thailand is not a very big nor a very rich country, but it is unique. It has a way of life that mixes ancient ritual with the ways of the modern world. Culture shock is everywhere: the Buddhist monk in his traditional robes rides pillion on a Japanese motor-bike, on the wall of a room whirring with computers hangs a shrine pungent with incense on which offerings of food have been laid. The contradictions are in the very environment: spectacular scenery vies with squalid slums, delicate stuccoed temples are overshadowed by the modernist concrete headquarters of multinational corporations. We have a centuries old Asian culture yet we turn willingly to the West for the latest fads and fashions. Sometimes it's hard, even for a Thai, to work out how this works and where it is going next.

Thailand is the central country of South East Asia, on the edge of what used to be French Indo-China. We have Burma to the west, Laos to the north, our querulous neighbour Cambodia to the east, to the south lies Malaysia. Although we have much in common with our neighbours we Thais are different. Our ancestors moved out of central and southern China about the ninth century possibly as a result of the Mongol invasions. At first they crossed Cambodia and entered the eastern part of what is now our country where they were subservient to the ruling Khmer empire. By the thirteenth century the Thai population was large enough to rebel against its distant Khmer rulers in their capital at Angkor Wat and to set up an independent kingdom centred on the city of Sukhothai which means, appropriately, the Dawn of Happiness.

Engraving of a Siamese war elephant

Previous page: King Mongkut of Siam (Rama IV), in ceremonial dress, the author's distant ancestor

Top: Gilded roofs of the Grand Palace, Bangkok. Left: Intricate, inlaid sculpture of Hanuman, the Monkey King, on the walls of the Grand Palace

complicated national institution with many families having at least one member involved. In a way it is almost a civil service as much as a fighting force and it ran the country fairly well. However, there has been considerable pressure for change in recent years and at last we now have an elected parliament even if many politicians are still soldiers in suits.

In recent times our national traumas have been occupation by the Japanese during the Second World War (with the building of the infamous Bridge over the River Kwai a short distance from Bangkok), and more recently the Vietnam War which led to Thailand being the main Rest and Recreation centre for American troops which turned areas of our major cities into

H.M. King Bhumiphol Adulyadej Rama IX, a twentieth-century monarch surrounded by ancient ceremonial

red light districts full of strip joints and massage parlours. Somehow we have survived all this and still remain independent and unique. Statistically we are poor, with appalling slums spreading around Bangkok as people are drawn to the boom city in search of illusory wealth, and yet it *is* a boom city with businesses flourishing and a growing middle class.

Despite all the problems of the modern world Thailand still has much of old Siam. Our present King, H. M. Bhumiphol Adulyadej Rama IX, is beloved for his good works and the fact that he has tried to nurture parliamentary control of the country. Much of village life remains unchanged with peasant farmers and simple fishermen still living in the elegant wooden stilt houses favoured by their ancestors. Even in the bustling cities there is still time for the delicate calm observance of religious duty – offering food to a begging monk, taking an offering of flowers and incense to a temple.

Although the typical Thai dwelling is a wooden house by a *klong* or stream, most Thais today dream of a modern house not much different from that seen in Europe or America. How could it be otherwise? The differences between peoples are far less than the similarities. And yet, when one of us has his modern house, with all its so-called amenities, the first thing we do is call in the monks to bless it and to set up our family statue of the Buddha beside which we place the images of our ancestors and so preserve the continuum of life that has held us together as a people ever since that distant migration centuries ago.

Of course many of our national characteristics have been lost, but oddly enough what survives has done so just because it is so strong even in the face of enormous pressure from Western-style films, music, fashions, television. Where else would you find a place that celebrates the opening of a bank, equipped with all the latest computerized technology, with the simultaneous opening of a model home, in traditional style, designed to house the dispossessed spirit of the land whose anger might result in all sorts of dreadful calamities? In any case, a mere half-hour's drive from Bangkok where the dying light plays on the flooded ricefields and a smiling child rides his tame water-buffalo home to his village, there is still a world of calm and wisdom unspoiled by the city dwellers' folly, where as the evening meal is set out and thanks are given for the blessings of the rice harvest that sustains rich and poor alike there is still that sense of community and dignity that the East has always cherished.

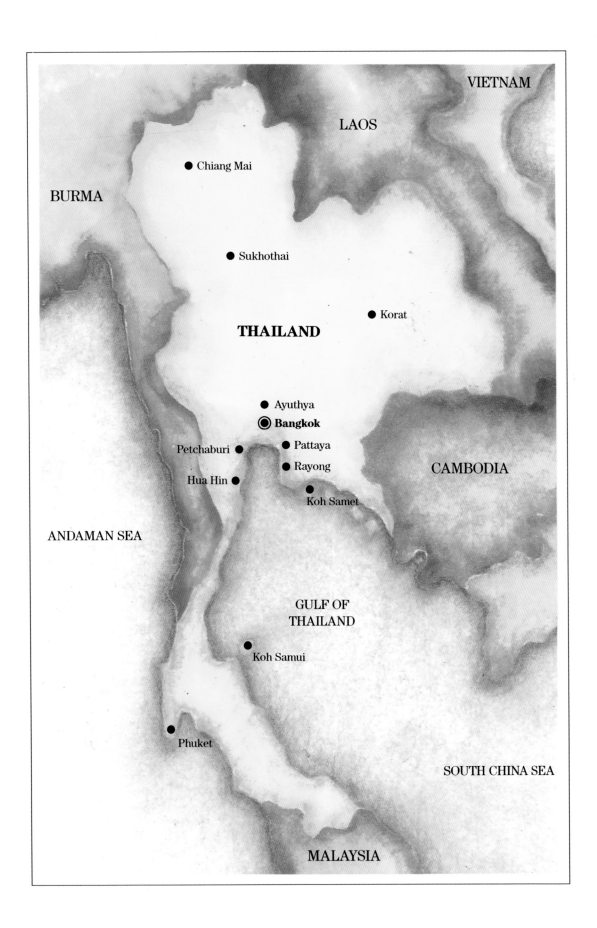

HOUSE & MARKET

AN INTRODUCTION TO THAI COOKING.
ESSENTIAL EQUIPMENT, INGREDIENTS
AND TECHNIQUES, DRINKS.
HOW TO USE THIS BOOK. MEASUREMENTS.

When I was a schoolboy we lived in Sala-daeng, then a pleasant tree-lined suburb on the outskirts of Bangkok beside which ran the Sathorn Klong or canal. In those days it was still possible to see flat-bottomed boats going to and from the Chao Phya River, then the city's main thoroughfare. Our house, like others in the neighbourhood, stood in its own garden, a two-storey brick and wood structure with an outside staircase to the first floor veranda in what was called the 'colonial' style because the fashion for such houses grew in the Chinese business community whose associates in Malaya had acquired a taste for the lifestyle of the British officials and settlers. It was a handsome building but despite its 'modern' look it had much in common with the traditional Thai stilt houses in the bright green paddy fields that were then only a short distance away from the city. Just like her country cousins, our cook, Kuhn Aat, worked in a wooden outhouse, sitting cross-legged on the ground as she chopped and sliced the vegetables or pounded the spices in a heavy stone mortar before tossing them all into the sizzling

19th century engraving of Thai ladies enjoying a meal

wok on the earthenware charcoal stove. My mother would prepare special dishes like *Nam Prik*, a pungent shrimp paste sauce that we all loved and which every Thai cook prepares in her own way, some adding baby eggplant, others adding more chilli. Mother saw to the presentation of the food, the decorative details and in all essentials, this was Thai cuisine as it had been for centuries, in equipment, methods and of course tastes. Today, in the countless hamlets that dot the Thai countryside, the old methods are still in use and when faced with this image of the traditional kitchen, with its ceramic bowls and wooden implements, the newcomer to Thai cooking may feel that this is all too removed from the realities of contemporary life. Until the Sixties this might have been so, but now Bangkok has changed – our 'colonial' house was pulled down twenty years ago and replaced by a modern concrete building, the sort of dwelling you see everywhere now. Open any Thai magazine and you'll see advertisements for the Ideal Home our young marrieds dream about, identical to the sort of suburban villas the middle classes want everywhere. We may deplore this standardization but then we don't have to squat on an earthen floor or cook on a charcoal brazier. At first our new home meant little difference to the food. We still had an outhouse and Kuhn Aat went on cooking much as before. The sparkling fitted-kitchen, with its cabinets, its refrigerator and gas cooker was initially more for display

Page 26: Floating market. Once to be found everywhere, such markets are gradually becoming less common

The following ingredients are used less often and need only be bought for special recipes. There are rarer ingredients, used only once or twice in the book; these are explained when they appear.

Pea aubergines

Aubergine or Eggplant In Thailand, we use varieties of eggplant not easily available in Europe or the US. The pea aubergine is, as its name suggests, the size of a pea or small marble, and the small green aubergine is about 1 in/2.5 cm in diameter. These can be found in some Chinese and specialist stores. Otherwise the yellow and black aubergines commonly found outside Asia may be substituted, cut down to the size of the green aubergine.

Banana Leaf This can be obtained in some oriental stores. We use it to make containers for steaming. The dishes which call for banana leaf containers may be cooked in individual bowls, instead.

Banana leaf

Basil, Holy and Sweet Fresh holy basil can be bought in oriental stores and is also available dried. It has a darker leaf than the European basil and a slightly aniseed, sharper flavour. If you are unable to find it, sweet basil may be substituted.

Bean Curd This can be bought in oriental stores, health food stores, and some supermarkets. It is usually in blocks of approximately 4 oz/100 g (and multiples) in its liquid, which is discarded. A 4 oz/100 g block will give 4 × 1 in/2.5 cm cubes. It is very delicate and won't last more than a couple of days in the refrigerator.

Fried bean curd is available pre-prepared in oriental stores.

Bean Curd Sheets These are bought dried in packets from oriental stores. They look rather like wrinkled brown paper and are extremely delicate in their dry state. To use them for

Bean curd sheet

wrapping they have to be soaked for 5-6 minutes to soften them, and while they tear easily, you can 'patch' with other pieces.

Red Bean Curd is available in 8 oz/230 g jars.

Bean Sauce Black bean, yellow bean and red bean sauces are equally salty and flavourful, and interchangeable: choice often depends on what would look more attractive in the dish. All are made from preserved soy beans and are usually available in bottles or jars.

Curry, Paste and Powder Several kinds of paste are used in Thai cuisine and most are available pre-prepared in foil packets. But it is much more satisfactory to make your own and recipes are given on p. 92-p. 93. When curry powder is stipulated in a recipe a pre-prepared mild Indian curry powder can be used.

Krachai

Dried Shrimp An ingredient frequently used in Thai dishes, both whole and ground. It can usually be found in Chinese and oriental stores in small packets.

Galangal

Galangal (Galanga, Galangale, Kha, Laos) This looks similar to ginger root, but has a more translucent skin and a pinkish tinge. It is peeled like ginger, but sliced rather than slivered. It is available fresh in oriental stores and can also be bought dried.

Ginger Always used in fresh root form and widely available. The root is first peeled and usually sliced thin, slivered, or diced very small.

Kaffir Lime This is roughly the same size and shape as the common lime but with a knobbly skin. The skin is often used, chopped, in recipes for curry paste. The skin of the common lime may be substituted.

Krachai Also known as lesser ginger, it is of the same family as ginger and galangal, though is a smaller root. It has a fiercer, wilder flavour than ginger. Sometimes available fresh in oriental stores, it can also be found dried in small packets and in this form should be soaked in water for 30 minutes before use.

Mushrooms The dried mushrooms called for in many of these recipes are usually called Dried Black Fungus or Champignon Noir, and can be bought in 2 oz/60 g packets. Buy the smallest variety available – avoiding any that are larger and coarser. For most recipes you will only need 6-7 pieces. When they are soft and pliable they can be cut into smaller pieces. Your 2 oz/60 g packet should be enough for 8-10 dishes. Straw and oyster mushrooms can be found conveniently in cans. Some dried mushrooms contain a high proportion of sandy grit and need to be checked carefully after soaking.

Oyster Sauce This is sold in bottles and is widely available.

Peanuts Ground roasted peanuts are frequently used, and can be bought whole and ground at home. Those easiest available will probably be salted, but this does not matter.

Preserved Turnip (Chi Po) This is used only in small amounts, usually chopped fine. Found in Chinese and oriental stores.

Preserved Radish (Tang Chi) This is often found whole or in slices, in vacuum-sealed packages from Chinese or oriental stores. We use it in small amounts, slivered or chopped, to add texture and flavour.

Rice Vinegar While most white vinegars can be used, I prefer the authenticity of the rice vinegar which is readily available in all Chinese and other specialist stores.

Carrying shallots to market

Shallots These are the small red onions usually found in Chinese and similar shops. European shallots can also be used, but if neither is available a small onion can be substituted.

Shrimp Paste This can be found in jars, tins and packages. Pungent and salty, it lasts very well and is used only in small amounts.

Spring Onion/Scallion This is a frequent ingredient in Thai dishes both as a flavouring and as a garnish and sliced in many different ways to enhance the appearance of a dish.

Tamarind

Tamarind The pulp of the fruit is exported in a compressed packaged form. To extract the juice or water, the pulp should be dissolved in hot water and the resulting liquid strained. It is quite sour and if it is not available lemon juice may be substituted in twice the amount of tamarind required.

Taro This rather bland-flavoured tuber is used as a vegetable or pulped to make a dessert with flavourings.

Turmeric Another member of the ginger family, this can occasionally be found fresh in oriental stores, but is more frequently available in powdered form.

Turmeric

BASIC TECHNIQUES

Chopping chillies

Home from marketing you are ready to begin. As I said earlier, the time you will have to spend actually cooking is quite small, which is why Thai food is ideal for the Western dinner party. But there is a price to pay for this: everything does have to be prepared in advance, and that means a lot of slicing, chopping and pounding to ensure that all the ingredients are lined up ready for the quick burst of cooking that you will finally do. There is a charming myth that because knives are a sign of aggression they are never seen at a Thai meal and that is why everything has to be cut down to a size that can be eaten on a spoon with rice. I don't know whether there is any truth in this – it is probably more accurate to say that only by cutting vegetables, meat and poultry into tiny segments can you both seal in their flavours and stir-fry them quickly in the oriental manner.

Basic techniques are:

Vegetable preparation In Thailand we prefer our ingredients prepared in as delicate a way as possible. So think small. Vegetables cut finely cook quickly and thus retain the maximum amount of their essential goodness. Garlic, shallots, ginger, chillies, etc., are very finely sliced, slivered or chopped. Hard vegetables, e.g. carrots and potatoes, are cut or sliced in small pieces; green vegetables such as broccoli are cut into small florets.

Stir-frying If you have ever cooked a Chinese meal you will be familiar with this method of cooking. It is simple and fast, but requires your constant attention. As its name implies, ingredients are stirred while being cooked: the stirring is, in fact, more a matter of turning the ingredients in the cooking oil or liquid to ensure that they are exposed to the heated medium. It is best achieved in a long-handled wok over high heat since you can manipulate the cooking vessel over the heat source. It is very fast and vegetables should be cooked in this manner only for a few seconds. They should remain crisp and bright-coloured.

Steaming Many dishes are steamed and a large steamer is a good investment. Steaming is timed from the moment the dish is placed over water already boiling in the lower section of the steamer and producing steam.

STOCK/BROTH

In the restaurant and at home, I make a stock from fresh chicken carcasses or from beef or pork bones, and water. No vegetables, herbs or spices are added. The carcasses or bones are covered with water, brought to boiling point, the heat immediately reduced, the liquid skimmed of any impurities which may have come to the surface as scum, and then simmered for at least two hours, skimming from time to time as necessary.

Commercial stock cubes are full of additional flavourings and should only be used as a last resort. Use water as an alternative. Another possibility is essence of chicken if available. This essence, is in a 2½ fl oz/70 ml jar and will turn to a jelly if left in the refrigerator. While quite expensive, it is highly concentrated and can be quite heavily diluted to make a light stock: 3 tsp/15 ml per cup of water; 2 tbs/30 ml per pt/570 ml.

And so to eat. The ideal balanced Thai meal has steamed rice, small bowls of clear soup for each diner, a steamed dish and a fried dish, a strong sauce usually with chillies used as a dip for vegetables and a salad often tossed with meat or fish. Dishes are not served as separate courses, everything is set out together and eaten as each diner wishes by simply dipping his or her spoon into which-ever is fancied and carrying a little back to his or her plate to be combined with the rice that has already been served there. Serving spoons are seldom used, eating is a shared matter and no one takes a large individual helping. You go on dipping in until you have had sufficient, not until you have dutifully cleared your plate. There should always be extra rice in case visitors drop in, formal invitations to dine are not usual in Thailand, and if someone comes it is thought better to run up some new dishes rather than make more of what has already been cooked – it is more *Sanuk*, that essential fun element we like so much.

Westerners who have patiently mastered the difficult art of eating with chopsticks often feel cheated when they discover that Thais only use them for eating noodles, which are of Chinese origin anyway. In the country, people often eat with their fingers, rolling the rice into a ball before dipping into the spicy flavourings. But for most of us, fork, spoon and plate are the norm. When our court was modelled on that of the Celestial Emperors, noble Thais did eat with chopsticks but when King Chulalongkorn began to modernize our country in the last century this brought not only universities and railways but also such Western fashions as long hair for women and the European style of dining. In the King's charming Victorian-style palace *The Viman-mek*, the pretty dining table is set out with French cut-glass and English porcelain stamped with the symbols of Thai royalty, and from there the habit spread.

The equipment may have changed but the form of the meal hasn't. There are no hors d'oeuvres as such but it is usual for those not involved in the cooking to have a drink, say whisky, while nibbling at snacks the returning workers have brought home with them: a little spicy sausage nibbled with cashew nuts and tiny cubes of fresh ginger, a pungent salad made from grated raw papaya tossed with fish sauce and mixed with tiny hot green chillies. To these will be added the dishes of the main meal, brought out as they are cooked so that they can be sampled with the drinks. When all the food has appeared the hostess will announce: '*Kin Khao*' – eat rice – and the meal proper will begin.

That is our way of doing it but as the major hotels in Thailand have shown, it is no problem to separate off some of these appetiz-ers, dips and salads as well as some of the smaller grilled dishes in order to make a first course. Soups and fish dishes can also make individual courses if required. It is up to the hosts – as long as the result is *Sanuk*, that's fine.

An everyday evening meal would normally be followed by fresh fruit. Thailand is famous for the high quality of its tropical fruits, and these would normally be peeled, sliced and neatly arranged on dishes before being offered to everyone; again that emphasis on sharing. If Thai sweets are served then ideally there should be two, one liquid, perhaps lotus seeds in coconut cream, and one dry, perhaps *Met Kanoon* made with egg, moong beans and sugar, and then fresh fruit last of all. After a full meal like that one's feelings should be *Sabai*, or well-being, the ultimate aim of all Thai activity.

In the heat of the kitchen

DRINKS

Iced tea brought to your boat – by boat!

The first-time visitor to a large Bangkok restaurant is always struck by the sight of diners arriving bearing bottles of whisky or brandy. A party out for the evening always takes its own drink, usually spirits, and this is then served, much iced and watered down, throughout the meal. This emphasis on spirits has reinforced the notion that Thai cuisine with its strong, hot flavours is not best accompanied by wine. To counter this, it is useful to know that the ancient Romans

Bangkok street vendor mixes fruit juice with crushed ice

flavoured their food with a liquid not unlike our fish sauce, that they were keen on strongly spiced dishes and yet drank wine with their meals. Of course, a delicate flavoured vintage would be somewhat wasted but any good robust wine goes well with anything other than the heavier curries. If you want to follow the Thai habit and stick with watered-down spirits, fair enough – there is even a Thai whisky 'Mekong', but it is not for the delicate! Other than that there is always lager and a Thai variety, 'Singha' is now sold abroad. For those who don't want alcohol suffice is to say that most Thais only drink water with their meals though a pleasant variant often found in Thailand is iced tea which is not only delicious but helps clear the palate.

ICED TEA

Cha Dam Yen

Dissolve sugar in boiling water to make a thin syrup. Make strong tea and allow to cool. Fill a tall glass with ice and add a slice of lemon, cover with tea and sweeten with syrup.

HOW TO USE THIS BOOK

Unless otherwise stated, all recipes are designed to make either:

A whole meal for one person
Part of a meal for two people with one other dish
Part of a meal for three people with three other dishes

In other words, portions are quite small, as it is the Thai custom to serve between three and five dishes at a meal, and if there are guests to add more dishes rather than just increase the amounts of what is already there.

In nearly all cases, cooking time is extremely short and it is therefore essential to have all your ingredients prepared and ready to hand before you begin.

MEASUREMENTS

I have not made any distinction between the UK and US measures of tablespoon and teaspoon – the differences are not vital to these recipes so long as the proportions are maintained by using the same spoon. They are always used as LEVEL measures. The metric equivalents of these measures are given as follows:

1 teaspoon (tsp)	=	5 ml
1 tablespoon (tbs)	=	15 ml

All equivalents have been rounded to the nearest convenient unit.

LIQUID MEASURES

1 US cup	=	8 fl oz	=	240 ml (approx. ¼l)
1 US pint	=	16 fl oz	=	475 ml
1 UK pint	=	20 fl oz	=	570 ml

DRY MEASURES

You will find that I have used metric liquid measures (millilitres) for solid substances (eg. sugar, curry paste) where the amounts used are small, ie. teaspoons and tablespoons. It is much more simple to measure such amounts in this way rather than weigh them. There is no difference between UK and US weight measures; convenient metric equivalents are given as:

1 oz	=	30g
4 oz	=	120g
8 oz	=	230g
1 lb	=	450g

US cup dry measures can only be given imperial and metric equivalents for specific substances (to the nearest convenient unit):

1 cup flour	= 5oz	= 145g
1 cup granulated sugar	= 8oz	= 240g
1 cup dessicated coconut	= 2½oz	= 75g
1 cup peanuts	= 5oz	= 145g
1 cup sweetcorn (drained)	= 5½oz	= 165g
1 cup dry rice	= 7oz	= 210g
1 cup cooked rice	= 8oz	= 240g

Hand-sorting shallots in the sun

REFLECTIONS IN A
FIELD OF WATER

COUNTRY COOKING
FIRST STAGES & ELEMENTARY DISHES

in-khao, 'eat rice', the Thai way of summoning guests to a meal reveals how that simple white grain lies to the heart of our cuisine. When we eat we take rice first and use all other dishes as flavours to help demolish the little mountain on the plate before us. A true Thai feels unsettled if he doesn't eat rice at least once a day and no one doubts that the rice farmer is the most important worker in the kingdom. The paddy fields of the central plains, watered by a complex web of ancient irrigation channels are the real Thailand. Rice is our foremost export and the wealth it has brought has fostered succeeding civilizations and city states, from the now ruined Sukhothai down to present day Bangkok. Beyond that noisy sprawling metropolis another, timeless culture still survives. Speeding from city to city in a fast car you only glimpse this other world, across a flooded paddy field you see a cluster of wooden houses nestling beside the red and gold brilliance of a village temple, home to a way of life where modernity has a light touch. Buffaloes graze by the side of the super-highway, across a narrow bank raised above the water a woman staggers under the weight of two yoked panniers filled with fruit, after the city the air is sweet.

Only forty minutes drive from the centre of Bangkok you move straight back into that other world. Near the little market town of Hua Ta Keh the paddies stretch to the horizon broken only by the tiny hamlets on the banks of the *klongs* that flow into the Chao Phya. In May the rains come and everyone must go to the flooding fields for the arduous task of transplanting the little green shoots. In their shell-like straw hats the figures bend calf-deep in the glistening sea as if plucking at their own reflections in a vast mirror. Nothing that they do has altered since rice was first cultivated in the river basins of Asia; the jet aircraft screaming overhead could be a visitor from another planet.

Early photograph of a village stilt-house by a klong

Page 44: Raking over the rice harvest to dry out before it is sent down to Bangkok

Steaming Thai sweets in a traditional kitchen by a klong

The dwellings here are not the stilt houses typical of much of Thailand. Here they live in low barn-like structures made of plaited bamboo-matting, the wide space covered with two pitched roofs. Here the farmer and all his family live with enough room for their buffalo. The farmer I visited recently no longer had an animal but shared the space with a rusting skeleton of a machine that he used for ploughing and which he called his 'mechanical buffalo'. His working day begins early and his wife starts to prepare food at five in the morning just before dawn. Instead of the traditional charcoal brazier she has an old metal stove that burns rice husks and a new electric rice-cooker, one of the few modern inventions of any use to her. For the rest, it is the usual display of metal pots and pans that you see stacked high in every market place. She cooks outside on a jetty washed by their *klong* from which her husband can dredge fish with a net on a frame not unlike a large broken umbrella. This is the most fertile part of the country and much of what they eat is freely to hand: many vegetables and herbs grow wild, others they cultivate on little plots near the house. In the busy planting season she often cooks only the most elementary Thai meal: boiled rice, a deep-fried fish served with her own version of the spicy *Nam Prik* sauce that is eaten everywhere in Thailand. When this simple meal is ready the family will not eat straight away, they are expecting a visitor and as the first light appears a long narrow boat is rowed into the *klong* by a monk in his vivid saffron robe. For the farmer and his wife this is the most important moment of their day, the placing of an offering of food in the alms bowl of their venerable visitor. It is a chance to uplift the spirit from the mundane tasks of the day by earning merit through giving.

With the coming of the rains and the rice safely planted,

*Village boys enter
their local
monastery during
the rainy season*

many of the young men of the village will become temporary
monks themselves. There will be an elaborate ceremony when
their heads are shaved and they are dressed in finery of white
fringed with gold, almost like brides, and are then carried
shoulder-high in procession to the temple. They will spend
three months purifying body and soul through prayer and
abstinence. The life of the farmer may be hard but it also has
great beauty. Few wish to change their lot as long as they can
provide food for their families. It is the impoverished people of
the dry north-east who leave the land for the dubious
advantages of the city. Perhaps with the city so near the
temptation is less. Just across the paddy is the King Mongkut
Institute of Technology where my brother teaches, it is home

FRIED MARINATED BEEF
Nua Cheh Nam Pla

2 tbs/30ml fish sauce
1 tsp/5ml salt
1 tsp/5ml sugar
1 tbs/15ml oil, plus 6 tbs/90 ml oil for frying
1 lb/450g skirt or flank beef, sliced diagonally across the grain into about 8-10 pieces

In a medium bowl mix the fish sauce, salt, sugar and 1 tbs/15ml oil. Add the pieces of beef and turn them thoroughly in the mixture. Leave to marinate for at least an hour. Remove the meat and drain on a rack. In Thailand, after marinating we would put the meat in the sun to dry: this can be simulated simply by leaving it overnight. If you wish to eat straight away, put the pieces of meat under a low grill or in a warm oven for about 10-15 minutes until dry. To finish, heat the oil in a frying pan until a very light haze appears and fry the meat on both sides until it is dark brown – about 5 minutes.

STEAMED EGG
Kai Toon

If you don't have a steamer, use a large lidded pan instead. Upturn a bowl in the bottom of the pan, add water to come about half-way up the upturned bowl and place the dish of eggs on top. Cover the pan and steam. Make sure the pan is large enough for you to remove the dish of cooked eggs easily.

3 large eggs
2oz/60g minced/ground pork
1 spring onion/scallion, trimmed and finely chopped
1 shallot, finely chopped
3 tbs/45ml fish sauce
1 tsp/5ml ground white pepper
1 tbs/15ml water
1 tsp/5ml finely chopped coriander leaf

Break the eggs into a deep bowl which can be easily removed from your steamer or pan. Add the pork, chopped spring onion and shallot, fish sauce, white pepper and water. Lightly beat together. Add the chopped coriander and stir. Place the bowl in the steamer or pan and steam for 12-15 minutes until the egg is set – test it with the tines of a fork; they should come out clean with no liquid on them.

Traditionally patterned material

SON-IN-LAW EGGS
Kai Look Koei

This dish is famous in Thailand as much for its name as its taste. 'Eggs', needless to say, is a euphemism!

6 eggs
oil for deep-frying, plus 2 tbs/30ml
1 small onion, finely sliced
4 tbs/60ml fish sauce
2 tbs/30ml sugar
½ tsp/2-3ml crushed dried chilli or chilli powder

Hard-boil/cook the eggs for 6-8 minutes. Rinse in cold water and shell. Heat the oil in the deep-fryer or wok until a light haze appears. Using a slotted spoon, lower the eggs into the oil and fry gently, turning carefully, until they are a light golden brown. Remove from the oil, drain, halve lengthways and arrange on a serving dish. Set aside.

In a small frying pan, heat the remaining oil until a light haze appears. Fry the sliced onion until crisp and deep brown. Remove from the pan with a slotted spoon, drain and set aside. There should be a film of oil left in the pan. Turn the heat down low and add the fish sauce, sugar and chilli. Cook slowly, stirring, until the sugar has dissolved. Continue to cook for about a minute until the mixture thickens, then add the reserved onions and stir for a few seconds to mix. Remove immediately from the heat, pour over the eggs and serve.

PICKLED CABBAGE
Prik Pak Dong

This pickle is easy to make and goes well with simple dishes. The 'pickling' is achieved by the action of the garlic, sugar and salt on the cabbage, forming a liquid. It will keep in an airtight jar in the refrigerator for 2-3 weeks, but no longer.

1 Chinese cabbage (Chinese leaves), about 2lbs/1kg
3 garlic cloves, finely chopped
2 large red chillies, finely chopped
1 tbs/15ml sugar
2 tbs/30ml salt

Cut the leafy top (about 1½-2in/4-5cm) from the cabbage and use it in another dish, or as a salad.

Trim away the base of the cabbage and cut the remainder into 2 in/5cm slices. Put into a large bowl, add the remaining ingredients and mix thoroughly. Spoon into a preserving or similar jar, seal the jar and leave for 3 days in a cool place (larder, pantry or refrigerator).

You now have enough recipes to create a full meal. Here are two suggested menus which you can shuffle around as you wish and which will adequately feed 3-4 people:

A
Rice
Chicken fried with chilli and nuts
Bean curd soup
Deep-fried spare-ribs
Son-in-law eggs
Pickled cabbage

B
Rice
Pork fried with ginger
Vermicelli soup
Fried marinated beef
Steamed egg

FRIED RICE WITH CHICKEN AND CURRY POWDER
Khao Pad Karee Gai

Separate from full meal dishes are those 'mopping-up' recipes that can provide lunch or a quick snack. Fried rice is the classic 'day-after' method of using up the extra rice from the night before. It is always a separate meal in Thailand; it would be rather eccentric to serve it in place of plain boiled rice as the staple for a dinner.

I suggest three recipes here but you can make up your own variations when you've mastered the technique. In all fried rice dishes, use less rather than more oil. The result should be dry, with the rice grains separate.

At a Bangkok rice warehouse

2 tbs/30ml oil
2 garlic cloves, finely chopped
2 tsp/10 ml medium-hot curry powder
3oz/90g boneless chicken, chopped or finely sliced
1 lb/450g/2½ cups cooked rice
1 tbs/15ml light soy sauce
2 tbs/15ml fish sauce
¼ tsp/1-2 ml sugar
1 spring onion/scallion, trimmed, and slivered into 1in/2½cm lengths
½ small onion, finely slivered
a shaking of ground white pepper

In a wok or frying pan, heat the oil until a light haze appears. Add the garlic and fry until golden brown. Add the curry powder, stir and cook for a few seconds; add the chicken and cook for a minute or two until the meat is opaque. Add the rice and stir thoroughly. Add the soy sauce, fish sauce and sugar, stirring after each addition. Cook together for a few seconds until you are certain that the meat is cooked and the rice thoroughly reheated. Turn onto serving dish, garnish with the spring onion, and onion, and lightly sprinkle with pepper.

PINEAPPLE-FRIED RICE
Khao Pad Supparot

I have included this as much for the chance it offers for a theatrical presentation as for any other reason. Using the whole, fresh pineapple as the serving dish looks marvellous and is really very easy. It is important to choose the pineapple carefully: it should be ripe, sweet and juicy.

1 pineapple
3 shallots, coarsely chopped
1 large red chilli, finely slivered
1 spring onion/scallion, green part only, coarsely chopped
1 sprig of coriander, coarsely chopped
2 tbs/30ml oil
2 tbs/30ml dried shrimp
2 garlic cloves, finely chopped
1 lb/450g/2cups cooked rice
1 tbs/15ml fish sauce
1 tbs/15ml light soy sauce
1 tsp/5ml sugar
coriander leaves, to garnish

Cut the pineapple in half lengthways. If the fruit is large, set one half aside to eat as dessert. Hollow the flesh out of both halves, chopping it into ½ in/1cm cubes. Put the pineapple flesh in a bowl, and add the shallots, chilli, scallion and coriander; mix and set aside.

In a wok or frying pan/skillet, heat 1 tbs/15ml oil, add the dried shrimp and fry until crispy. With a slotted spoon, remove the shrimp, drain and set aside. Add the remaining 1 tbs/15ml oil, heat, add the garlic and fry until golden brown. Add the cooked rice, stir thoroughly. Add the fish sauce, soy sauce and sugar. Stir and mix thoroughly. Make sure the rice is heated through, then add the pineapple mixture and the crispy shrimp. Mix all thoroughly and heat through. Fill the pineapple shell(s) with the mixture, garnish with a little more coriander and serve.

FRIED RICE WITH PRAWN AND CHILLIES
Khao Pad Prik Gung

2 tbs/30ml oil
2 garlic cloves, finely chopped
2 small red chillies, finely chopped
4oz/120g peeled prawns
1 tbs/15ml fish sauce
¼ tsp/1-2ml sugar
1 tbs/15ml light soy sauce
1 lb/450g/2½ cups cooked rice
½ small onion, slivered
½ red or green sweet pepper, slivered
½ tsp/2.5ml ground white pepper
1 spring onion/scallion, green part only, slivered into 1in/2½ cm lengths
coriander leaves, to garnish

In a wok or frying pan, heat the oil until a light haze appears. Add the garlic and fry until golden brown. Add the chillies and the prawns and stir quickly. Add the fish sauce, sugar and soy sauce; stir and cook for a few seconds until the prawns are cooked through. Add the cooked rice and stir thoroughly. Add the onion, sweet pepper, white pepper and spring onion and stir quickly to mix. Turn onto a serving dish and garnish with the coriander leaves.

CITY OF ANGELS

BANGKOK LIFE
MORE ADVANCED FOOD

1 n the darkness three linked rice barges plough down the Chao Phya, low in the water. A light flickers at the stern of the forward vessel – the cooking fire of the family for whom this is a permanent home. They pass through the centre of old Bangkok, past rickety wooden houses built out into the river on stilts, past the green-tiled roofs and golden spires of the Grand Palace, and the Temple of the Emerald Buddha, Thailand's national shrine. On the opposite bank, in Thonburi, the tallest spire of all, Wat Arun, the Temple of the Dawn, appropriately catches the first light which plays on the vivid shards of Chinese pottery used to make its dazzling mosaic shell. King Taksin, the Chinese General who saved the Thai nation after our defeat by the Burmese in the eighteenth century, set up his headquarters in Thonburi while he drove the invaders from our land. It was his successor King Rama I who moved the capital to its present site and gave it the name we use – Krung Thep, the City of Angels. Early foreign visitors used the name of the nearby port – Bangkok, 'place of the wild

Early engraving of The Temple of the Dawn

Previous pages: The Temple of the Dawn seen across the Chao Phya river

beef and stir thoroughly. Add the soy sauce, fish sauce, sugar, lime leaves and stock. Cook for a minute or two over a high heat, stirring all the time and mixing thoroughly. Add the red pepper, green beans and white pepper and stir for 4-5 seconds. Turn onto a serving dish.

STUFFED OMELETTE
Kai Yat Sy

Although we call this an omelette it is really more like a filled crêpe. The taste leans towards sweetness so it must be served with something very savoury, such as the preceding beef dish. Taste aside, the real pleasure of this omelette is its unusual box-shape from which its colourful contents spill out when it is cut. It is worth having one or two practice runs at this dish to make sure it will succeed and impress your guests. It is easier to make in a wok than in a frying pan.

Filling:
1 tbs/15ml oil
1 garlic clove, finely chopped
2oz/60g minced/ground pork
about 1 tbs finely chopped carrot
about 1 tbs finely chopped onion
about 1 tbs finely chopped green beans
about 1 tbs finely chopped sweet red pepper
about 1 tbs finely chopped green pepper
1 small tomato, finely chopped
1 tbs/15ml peas (frozen will do)
2 tbs/30ml fish sauce
1 tbs/15ml light soy sauce
1 tbs/15ml tomato ketchup/catsup
½ tsp/2.5ml ground white pepper
Omelette:
2 eggs
1 tbs/15ml fish sauce
ground white pepper
1 tbs/15ml oil
coriander leaves and slivers of red and green pepper, to garnish

Make the filling. In a wok, heat the oil, add the garlic and fry until golden brown. Add the pork, and fry until the meat is white and opaque. Quickly add all the chopped vegetables and stir once. Add the fish sauce, soy sauce, tomato ketchup and pepper, and stir-fry over a high heat for 1 minute. Turn the mixture into a dish and set aside.

Clean the wok with kitchen paper. In a small bowl lightly beat the eggs with the fish sauce and a shake of white pepper. Heat the oil in the wok, tilting it over the heat to cover the inner surface with a fine film of hot oil. Add the beaten egg and tilt the wok to cover as much of the inner surface as possible with a thin layer of the egg mixture. Leave to cook for a few seconds to form a 'crêpe' and, when it is firm enough to hold its shape, tip the reserved filling into the centre. With a spatula fold the sides of the crêpe over the filling to form a square package. Slide onto a serving plate and garnish with coriander leaves and red and green pepper slivers.

MILLION-YEAR-EGGS
Tom Kem

This is that rare thing, a Thai stew – a dish that actually improves for being kept and re-heated. When I was a student in London it was one of the few Thai dishes I could find the ingredients for and I used to produce it in large quantities. Seeing it come back time and again my friends dubbed it 'million-year-eggs', the name I have given it here. It is obviously a useful standby and good for parties.

5 garlic cloves, finely chopped
2 coriander roots, finely chopped
½ tsp/2.5ml coarsely ground black pepper
1 tbs/15ml oil
1½lbs/700g belly pork cut into 1in/2.5cm cubes
1½-2pts/750-950ml stock/broth or water
2 tbs/30ml dark soy sauce
3 tbs/95ml fish sauce
2 tbs/30ml sugar
6 hard-boiled/cooked eggs, shelled
4 × 1in/2.5cm cubes fried bean curd (p.37), halved
Serves 6

Pound together the garlic, coriander roots and ground black pepper in a pestle and mortar, or grind in a blender. In a large heavy saucepan heat the oil and fry this mixture for 1 minute. Add the chunks of pork and fry for a minute or two, turning the pieces to absorb some of the mixture. Add enough stock or water to cover the mixture by 1in/2.5cm and bring to the boil. Skim off any impurities that come to the surface. Add the soy sauce, fish sauce and sugar. Add the hard-boiled eggs and simmer gently for an hour, skimming if necessary. The eggs should acquire a dark brown colour. Add the bean curd and cook for a few minutes longer.

A well-fed traffic warden, Bangkok

NAM PRIK, MY MOTHER'S STYLE
Nam Prik Kapee

Nam prik (literally, 'hot' or spicy water) is a Thai staple; a liquid paste into which raw vegetables, cold cooked vegetables and deep-fried fish are dipped and eaten with rice. This is another of those real tastes of Thailand, and is based on fermented ingredients which have a pungent smell that the newcomer may find unappealing. It's a question of holding your nose and eating – once you enjoy the taste you'll ignore the smell.

Every region of Thailand has its own versions of *Nam prik*, and indeed every Thai cook has his or her own special recipe – there will be others later on in this book. Traditionally, a Thai lady made her *Nam prik* while her servants got on with the main cooking, so the dish has acquired the status of an offering even though it is eaten frequently and isn't reserved for special occasions. The pea aubergines/eggplant we use in this sauce are rarely available in the West; they really are the size of peas or small marbles. You could use larger aubergines, 1-1½in/2.5-4cm in diameter, instead, but they are not essential.

This recipe is my mother's favourite.

2 garlic cloves, chopped
5 small hot chillies
1 tbs/15ml shrimp paste
3 tbs/45ml fish sauce
3 tbs/45ml lemon juice
1 tbs/15ml sugar
2 tbs/30ml crushed pea aubergines/eggplant, if available
To serve:
crudités (French/snap beans cut into 2in/5cm lengths, slivers of carrot, celery and cucumber) or
1 pomphret or 3 fresh sardines, cleaned (if available), plus oil for deep frying

Using a pestle and mortar or a blender, pound the garlic with the chillies. Gently grill the shrimp paste for 2 or 3 minutes (this may not be necessary in the West but we do it to destroy any bacteria that may have developed in our much hotter weather). Add the shrimp paste to the garlic and chilli mixture, blend, then add the rest of the ingredients and mix thoroughly. Serve with crudités. If you have a pomphret or sardines, deep fry the former and grill/broil the latter until quite dry and crisp, so that diners can scrape the flesh from the spine to dip in the *Nam prik*.

NOODLES/GUEYTEOW

This is the branch of Thai cuisine closest to Chinese cooking. If it is true that Marco Polo took the idea of pasta back to Italy, then he rather lost his sense of time on the long journey home, for whereas spaghetti, fuselli, etc. take several minutes to cook, oriental noodles take seconds. The time-consuming part is preparing all the other ingredients before you start so that they are ready literally to be flung into the pan for the small amount of cooking required.

There are five varieties of noodle, four made from rice flour and one from soya-bean flour. In most Thai noodle dishes, the protein element comes in the form of pre-prepared meat or fish balls. All these ingredients, both noodles and prepared meats, are available in Chinese stores and are exactly the same as those used in Thailand, where buying ready-made ingredients of this sort is standard practice.

Some Chinese supermarkets now stock fresh noodles which, especially in the case of egg noodles, are an improvement on the dried variety. The only difference in cooking is that the dried noodles should be soaked in water for a short time before they are used.

Apart from dividing by variety of noodle used, these dishes can be separated into dry and wet ones; that is, into fried noodle dishes or soup noodle dishes. A standard Thai lunch is often a bowl of soup noodle followed by a bowl of fried noodle. In some cases, soup noodle is made simply by adding stock/broth to the dry noodle.

The most famous dish of all is Pad Thai – a fried noodle with a complex set of ingredients that are mixed together by the diner. The flavour of Pad Thai is one of the most evocative in Thai cuisine and this gives it some claim to be the national dish.

FIVE NOODLES

1. Sen Yai Sometimes called River Rice Noodle or Rice Sticks, this is a broad, flat, white noodle. Bought fresh, it is rather sticky and the strands usually need to be separated by hand before cooking. Can also be bought dried.

2. Sen Lek A medium flat noodle, about $1/10$ in/2mm wide, and usually sold dried.

Making fresh river rice noodles

3. Sen Mee A small wiry-looking rice noodle, usually sold dried, sometimes called 'rice vermicelli'.

4. Ba Mee An egg noodle, medium yellow in colour, which can be bought fresh in 'nests'; these need to be shaken loose by hand before cooking.

5. Wun Sen A very thin, very wiry, transparent soya-bean-flour noodle, called either vermicelli, or 'cellophane noodle'. Only available dried.

All dried noodles need to be soaked in cold water for about 20 minutes before cooking; (vermicelli will usually require less soaking). They are quickly drained in a sieve or colander, and then cooked; usually a matter of simply dunking them into boiling water for 2-3 seconds. The dry weight will usually double after soaking, ie. 4oz/120g dry noodles are equivalent to 8oz/230g soaked noodles.

FOUR FLAVOURS
Kruang Prung

While each noodle dish has a distinctive flavour of its own, the final taste is left very much up to the consumer. When eating noodles in Thailand, it is standard practice to offer a set of four flavours: chillies in fish sauce/*Nam Pla Prik* (4 small green or red chillies to 4 tbs/60ml fish sauce), chopped chillies in rice vinegar/*Prik Nam Som* (4 small green or red chillies to 4 tbs/60ml vinegar), sugar/*Nam Tan* and red chilli powder/*Prik Pon*, so that the dish can be adjusted as the diner wishes.

RIVER NOODLES WITH PORK AND DARK SOY
Pad Si Yew

1 tbs/15ml oil
2 garlic cloves, finely chopped
4oz/120g minced/ground lean pork
1 egg
8oz/230g (wet weight) soaked *Sen Yai* noodles (p. 85)
2oz/60g broccoli, coarsely chopped
1 tbs/15ml dark soy sauce
1 tbs/15ml light soy sauce
pinch of sugar
2 tbs/30ml fish sauce
ground white pepper
chilli powder (optional)

Heat the oil in a wok or frying pan over a high heat. Add the garlic and fry until golden brown. Add the pork, stir, and cook briefly until the meat is opaque. Break the egg into the mixture, stir, and cook quickly. Add the noodles and stir quickly; add the broccoli and stir again to blend. Stirring quickly after each addition, add the dark soy, the light soy, the sugar, and the fish sauce. Give the mixture a final stir, turn onto a serving dish, shake the ground white pepper over, and the chilli powder if liked, and serve.

PORK AND FISH BALL NOODLES
Gueyteow Heng Moo

This is quite bland, and *must* be served with side dishes of the four flavours.

2 tbs/30ml oil
2 garlic cloves, finely chopped
1 tsp/5ml preserved radish (*tang chi*, p. 39)
1 tbs/15ml fish sauce
1 tbs/15ml light soy sauce
½ tsp/2.5ml sugar
1oz/30g beansprouts
8oz/230g (wet weight) soaked *Sen Yai* noodles (p. 85), rinsed and separated
3 prepared pork balls
3 prepared fish balls
4 slices prepared fish cake
4 slices cold boiled pork
1 tbs/15ml crushed roasted peanuts, plus extra to serve if wished
1 sprig of coriander leaves, coarsely chopped

Duck farm outside Bangkok to supply the restaurants of Chinatown

In a small bowl mix the first six ingredients together and set aside. Combine the sauce ingredients in a bowl and whisk/beat with a fork until smooth. Set aside.

In a saucepan bring the stock quickly to the boil. Add the reserved chicken mixture, stir quickly and cook for 1 or 2 minutes until the meat is opaque. Add the vegetables, fish sauce and soy sauce, and stir. Add the vermicelli, still stirring, and cook for 2 or 3 seconds: the noodles become soft very quickly. Turn into a bowl. Serve the sauce separately as it has a strong flavour: allow each diner to stir it in as required (I suggest you start with ½ tsp/ 2.5ml).

THAI FRIED NOODLES
Pad Thai

The total cooking time for this dish shouldn't exceed 2-3 minutes.

4 tbs/60ml oil
2 garlic cloves, finely chopped
1 egg
4 oz/120g dry *Sen Lek* noodles (p. 85), soaked in water for 20 minutes until soft, and drained
2 tbs/30ml lemon juice
1½ tbs/22.5ml fish sauce
½ tsp/2.5ml sugar
2 tbs/30ml chopped roast peanuts
2tbs/30ml dried shrimp, ground or pounded
½ tsp/2.5ml chilli powder
1 tbs/15ml finely chopped preserved turnip (*chi po*, p. 38)
1oz/30g beansprouts
2 spring onions/scallions, chopped into 1in/2.5cm pieces
sprig of coriander leaf, coarsely chopped
lemon wedges, to garnish

In a wok or frying pan, heat the oil, add the garlic and fry until golden brown. Break the egg into the wok, stir quickly and cook for a couple of seconds. Add the noodles and stir well, scraping down the sides of the pan to ensure they mix with the garlic and egg. One by one, add the lemon juice, fish sauce, sugar, half the peanuts, half the dried shrimp, the chilli powder, the preserved turnip, 1 tablespoon of the beansprouts, and the spring onions, stirring quickly all the time. Test the noodles for tenderness. When done, turn onto a serving plate and arrange the remaining peanuts, dried shrimp and beansprouts around the dish. Garnish with the coriander and lemon wedges.

CURRY/KARI

Chillies drying in the sun with stone mortars ready for pounding

Earlier, I mentioned the Thai tradition of making curry pastes at home rather than buying them. While this is time-consuming it is well worth the effort. I find it easier to spend a whole day making several pastes at once, all of which will be used in the coming two or three weeks.

In Thailand, we would use a heavy stone pestle and mortar for making curry pastes. As a substitute, I suggest you use either an electric coffee-grinder (because of the pungent flavours you will have to keep a grinder uniquely for this purpose), or buy pre-ground spices, such as coriander, cumin, etc. and use an electric blender to mix them in. If you want to try your hand at the traditional method, I suggest you pound all the 'hard' ingredients (cloves, coriander and cumin seeds, star anise, etc.) first, as these take most effort, and then add the remaining ingredients. There are many Thai curries; here I have chosen four that are very different in taste. After explaining the pastes, I give examples of how to use them: substitute other meats and vegetables for those I have suggested if you prefer.

Unlike Indian curries, Thai ones do not require long cooking, only a few minutes once the ingredients are prepared and ready to hand – like all Thai dishes. Our curries are also less 'thickened' than Indian ones; they are often more like a heavily spiced soup than a savoury dish. Ready-made curry pastes can be bought in Chinese and oriental stores. They make a convenient alternative, but are never as good as the homemade variety.

If you are using whole seeds to obtain the ground powder, first grind these separately in a blender or coffee grinder.

GREEN CURRY PASTE
Gaeng Kiow Wan

2 long green chillies, chopped
10 small green chillies, chopped
1 tbs/15ml chopped lemon grass
3 shallots, chopped
2 tbs/30 ml chopped garlic (about 4 cloves)
1in/2.5cm piece galangal, chopped
3 coriander roots, chopped
1 tsp/5ml ground coriander seed
½ tsp/2.5ml ground cumin
½ tsp/2.5ml ground white pepper
1 tsp/5ml chopped kaffir lime skin (p. 38) or finely chopped lime leaves (p. 36)
2 tsp/10ml shrimp paste
1 tsp/5ml salt

Using a pestle and mortar or a grinder, blend all the ingredients together until they form a smooth paste. These amounts will yield about 3 tbs/45ml paste.

A traditional coconut grater in the form of a rabbit

the warmed coconut cream (reserving 1 tbs/ 15ml for garnish), and stir until it curdles and thickens in the oil. Add the fish sauce and sugar and stir. Add the beef, stir and cook gently for 3-4 minutes. Add the lime leaves and stir in, then add the basil leaves. Cook for 1 minute. This is meant to be a dry curry, but add a little water during the cooking if you feel it is drying out too much. When the beef is cooked through, turn the mixture onto a serving dish and garnish with the reserved coconut cream and the slivers of red chilli.

THAI MUSLIM CURRY
Massaman Kari

The extreme south of Thailand, along our narrow border with Malaysia, has a largely Muslim population. From them we have acquired the satay sauce and this rich, though mild, curry. You can give it more fire by increasing the amount of paste you use. This curry needs to 'stew' a little.

8fl oz/250ml/1cup coconut cream
2 tbs/30ml oil
1 garlic clove, finely chopped
1 tbs/15ml Massaman curry paste (p. 93)
6oz/180g lean beef, cubed
1 tbs/15ml tamarind juice, or 2 tbs/30ml lemon juice
1 tsp/5ml sugar
3 tbs/45ml fish sauce
8fl oz/250ml/1cup stock/broth or water
2 small potatoes, quartered
2 tbs/40g roasted peanuts
2 small onions, quartered

In a small pan, gently warm the coconut cream until it just starts to separate. In a wok or frying pan/skillet, heat the oil, add the garlic and fry until golden brown. Add the curry paste, mix well and cook for a few seconds. Add half the warmed coconut cream, stir thoroughly to mix and, still stirring, cook for a further few seconds until the mixture bubbles and starts to reduce. Add the beef and turn to ensure that each piece of meat is thoroughly coated with sauce. Stirring after each addition, add the tamarind or lemon juice, sugar, fish sauce, stock or water and the remainder of the coconut cream. Stir and cook slowly for 15 minutes. Add the quartered potatoes and simmer. After 4 minutes, add the peanuts and cook for 4 minutes more. Add the onions, stir and cook for 2 more minutes. Turn into a serving dish.

SIDE-DISHES

The pickle stall in Wararot market, Chiang Mai. Not only vegetables but fruits like mango are preserved in rice vinegar

We usually balance the rich flavours of a curry with side-dishes that have lighter, sharper or sweeter tastes. You could serve 'Son-in-law eggs' (p. 61) or Pickled Cabbage (p. 62) with curries, and here are three more accompaniments.

PICKLED GARLIC
Kratiem Dong

Some of the early Western visitors to Siam were critical of the amounts of pickled garlic that were eaten. It is certainly an acquired taste and one best shared with close companions!

At home we pickle whole bulbs of garlic (which are smaller than the Western variety), and they look very pleasing in their pickling jars. Western garlic is too big for this treatment, so you will have to break it up into cloves. A little of this goes a long way.

2 large whole garlic bulbs, separated into cloves and peeled
¾pt/250ml white rice vinegar
2 tsp/10ml sugar
2 tsp/10ml salt

Place the peeled garlic cloves in a small preserving jar. Heat the vinegar with the sugar and salt until the sugar and salt are dissolved. Allow the mixture to cool. Pour the liquid over the garlic, seal the jar and leave for 1 week.

SALTY EGGS
Kai Kem

This is so easy to make and it makes a deliciously salty side-dish – the direct opposite of Son-in-law eggs.

8-9 eggs (duck eggs are preferred, but large chicken eggs are quite satisfactory)
10oz/300g/1cup salt
1¼pt/700ml/3cups water

Place the eggs, being careful not to crack the shells, in a 4pt/2l (or larger) preserving jar. Heat the salt and water together in a pan until the salt is dissolved. Allow to cool, and then pour the mixture over the eggs in the jar. Seal the jar and leave for 3 weeks after which the eggs can be boiled or fried.

SWEET CRISPY NOODLE

Mee Krop

This dish brings the noodle and curry sections together. I cannot pretend that it is anything other than a very complex dish – one of the most time-consuming in the book – but it does contain a unique blend of tastes and textures. It is the perfect accompaniment to a green or red curry, and, if you make it once I am sure you will come back to it again and again. Happily, it can be made a little in advance of a meal so that you don't have to go through all these rather finnicky stages right up to the time of eating.

oil for deep frying
4oz/120g dry *Sen Mee* noodles (p. 86), soaked in cold water for 20 minutes, and drained
Sauce:
2 tbs/30ml oil
2 × 1in/2.5cm cubes prepared fried bean curd (p. 37), cut or shredded into thin strips
2 tbs/30ml oil
2 garlic cloves, finely chopped
2 shallots, finely chopped
1oz/30g minced/ground pork
2 tbs/30ml fish sauce
4 tbs/60ml sugar
4 tbs/60ml stock/broth
3 tbs/45ml lemon juice
½ tsp/2.5ml chilli powder
Additions:
2 tbs/30ml oil
1 egg, lightly beaten with 1 tbs/15ml cold water
1oz/30g beansprouts
1 spring onion/scallion, cut into 1in/2.5cm slivers
1 medium-size red chilli, deseeded and slivered lengthways

Heat the oil in a deep-fryer until medium-hot. In two batches, fry the drained noodles until they are golden brown and crisp. Remove from the fryer, drain, and set aside.

In a wok or frying pan, heat the 2 tbs of oil, add the shredded bean curd, and fry until crispy. Remove with a slotted spoon and set aside. Reheat the oil, add the garlic and fry until golden brown; remove and set aside. Next fry the shallot until brown, remove and set aside. Then fry the pork until cooked through. Stirring, add the fish sauce, sugar, stock, and lemon juice. Stir the mixture until it begins to caramelize. Add the chilli powder and stir. Stir in the reserved bean curd, garlic and shallot, and mix until they soak up some of the sweet liquid. Set aside.

In a small pan, heat the remaining 2 tbs of oil. Drip in the egg mixture from the tips of the fingers; it will cook immediately, making little scraps of egg. Remove, drain, and set aside.

Return the wok or pan containing the sauce to the heat. Crumble the crisp vermicelli into the sauce, mix gently, and cook together briefly. Turn into a serving dish and sprinkle the beansprouts, spring onion, fried egg pieces and chilli over the mixture.

Embroidered cloth in traditional design

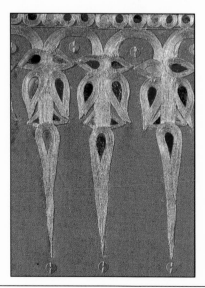

BY THE SEA

SEAFOOD

olidays at the seaside hold the same attractions for Thai children as for those of any other land: swimming, building sand-castles, beach football. I, however, always found greatest pleasure in walking alone for hours down an endless strand of white beach. I liked to stop and stare into a rock pool, watching a creature tentatively peep out of its shell, and I was always amused by the near transparent ghost-crabs scuttling sideways, as if turning cartwheels, before diving into their impossibly tiny holes in the sand. The only things which ever worried me were the giant jelly-fish, washed into the shallows during the rainy season. These monsters could be found on the beach when the tide went out and I would sometimes pick them up with two sticks to throw them out of reach of the sea, so that there would be one less danger for swimmers.

As a child I would stay at my great aunt's house at Hua Hin, a beach resort a half-day's drive from Bangkok, on the western shore of the Gulf of Thailand. As the daughter of a prince, it was almost obligatory that my great-aunt should have her holi-day house in Hua Hin which, since the Twenties, had been a second home for the Thai nobility. The region around Hua Hin had known royal visitors since the last century, but it was the construction of the railway link between the capital and Malaya, after the First World War, that put the sleepy seaside town within a four-hour train journey of Bangkok. In 1926 King Rama VII began work on his villa, Klai Kangwan, 'Far from worries', and this brought in its wake beach bungalows built by princes, princesses, and other court officials in the then fashionable style of English suburban bungalows. Visitors could stay at the Railway Hotel, a fairy-tale construction of wooden verandas with Victorian-style fret-work awnings, with topiary hedges carved into the shapes of animals apparently grazing on the well-watered lawns.

The king was to discover that 'Far from worries' was hardly the most appropriate name for his new residence for, in 1932, word came that there had been a revolution in Bangkok. Overnight His Majesty had been transformed from an absolute to a constitutional monarch. None of this affected Hua Hin which spent the next thirty years as a pleasant place for the well-to-do, away from any unrest in the capital. The town remained the country's principal resort until the Thai government started actively to promote tourism about twenty years ago. This led to the booming growth of Pattaya as the Miami Beach of South East Asia, a gaudy promenade of sky-scraper hotels, discos, massage parlours and international restaurants on the opposite side of the Gulf from sleepy old Hua Hin. The tourists have flocked to Pattaya. European ladies bare their breasts by the swimming pools, Arabs from the more

Prince Chula on holiday in Hua Hin in 1952

Page 100: Sun-dried fish, excellent for soup; hot and sour salad or with a spicy Nam Prik sauce

puritan parts of Islam come to enjoy the sins of the flesh, and every nationality can be found along its garish neon-lit main street, out for the evening stroll.

The more discriminating visitor has had to go further round the Gulf to enjoy the real pleasures of Thailand's coast, its wide deserted beaches and its simple fisher-folk life. Until ten years ago, those in the know made the journey to the island of Phuket, off the western side of the narrow isthmus that divides Thailand from Malaysia. Set in the Andaman Sea, the island offered simple accommodation in beach-side huts and the pleasures of freshly-caught fish and lobster grilled on an open fire. Nearby was Phangnga Bay, one of the world's most extraordinary natural beauty spots, a seascape dotted with surreal limestone outcrops; thin yet dizzyingly tall, rising dramatically out of the placid green waters. Built out into the bay on stilts, a fishing village offered wonderful food in a setting of breath-taking beauty. Too good to last, for in 1979 an international airport was opened and the hotels began to spring up. However, there is no need to despair, Thailand has many islands, and the adventurous can always keep one jump ahead of the builders. Today, young travellers backpack their way to the island of Koh Samui or continue down the coast from Pattaya to Koh Samet, a journey which takes them to the town of Rayong – famous as the main centre for the most essential ingredient in Thai food, fish sauce. There's no

Phangnga Bay, surrealist limestone outcrops rising from the sea. Now popular with tourists staying on the Island of Phuket

mistaking it, the whole place smells of drying fish. To offset the odour is the intriguing sight of thousands of pinkly translucent squid hung on lines to dry in the sun, like hosts of strange butterflies caught in gossamer nets.

While new resorts like Pattaya were springing up Hua Hin still remained largely unchanged. There was the addition of one or two more modern beach houses built by successful companies to provide weekend rest for their tired executives, but overall it was felt that the brasher aspects of the tourist trade should not infringe on the Royal Family's holiday home. A few miles to the north, at Cha'am, a modern hotel was built, but it is so neatly secluded from the old town that most of the tourists who stay there do not know that a short distance from where they are staying is a piece of fantasy well worth finding – near the local army barracks, right on the beach is a pleasure house built by King Rama VI, a series of airy wooden rooms on stilts, linked by walkways and verandas, one of which goes on out into the sea like an English pier. This was a place for parties and dalliance. Until recently, no one seemed to be responsible for looking after it and it was slowly crumbling away. It had the look of a haunted palace, a place of dreams, the only visitors an occasional group of young people who had ignored the warnings and clambered out onto the pavilion above the water to eat a picnic, play music, and laze an afternoon away. Happily, a decision has now been made to try to restore this magical place.

Today, Hua Hin's atmosphere of gentle decay may be ending. Faded scions of the older aristocracy still come for their holidays but the place has acquired a new smartness among the sophisticated young, who are drawn to its old-world charms. Change has been modest. The old Railway Hotel was spruced up with a coat of paint for its role as the Phnom Penh Hotel in the film *The Killing Fields*, and in 1986 the French Sofitel chain with their Thai partners undertook a sensitive restoration, keeping all the Thirties' fittings, so that the pleasures of the past have been improved by only the barest touches of modernity. My only complaint is that they have not kept the old name 'The Railway Hotel', with its nostalgic image of pre-war travel. However, as we Thais believe that your luck is improved if you walk under an elephant, so for me the best way to savour Hua Hin is still to enter the hotel by its gardens, passing under an enormous bush shaped like an elephant. In the foyer of the hotel one can admire a photograph of Miss Thailand 1940, and look into cabinets displaying the porcelain and silverware once used by the old Siamese Railways – worth more than a glance. After an aperitif you can ride in a *samloh* (a bicycle rickshaw) to the jetty, brightly flood-lit, where the larger motorized fishing boats have anchored. These are manned by tough deep-sea sailors, their arms blue with protective tattoos depicting religious or magical symbols. These wiry men live dangerously, often staying out for at least three days and nights at a time. The haul they bring is huge, a

A dried fish stall: hard sun-dried prawns and crispy wafers of squid

GRILLED FISH WITH CORIANDER AND GARLIC

Pla Pow

This is one of the simplest fish dishes. At home we wrap the fish in banana leaves and cook it on an open charcoal fire. Some Chinese supermarkets do stock banana leaves, so this method might be possible, but you can also use aluminium foil instead, and use your ordinary grill/broiler. Serve this with the sauce that accompanies Barbecued Seafood, (p. 112).

6 coriander roots
3 large garlic cloves
ground white pepper
1 mackerel or whiting, cleaned and patted dry inside and out
lettuce leaves, to garnish

Pre-heat the barbecue or grill/broiler.

With a pestle and mortar or blender, pound or grind the coriander roots and garlic together to form a paste and mix in a generous shaking of ground white pepper. Put this paste in the cavity of the cleaned fish. Wrap the fish in a banana leaf or foil; if using a banana leaf, simply roll the wide leaf around the stuffed fish, fold the ends over and secure the package with toothpicks. Grill/broil the fish for about 6-8 minutes each side. To serve, simply unwrap the fish and place on a bed of lettuce.

STEAMED FISH WITH GINGER AND MUSHROOMS

Pla Nung King

1 pomfret or similar fish, cleaned, and scored 2-3 times on each side
1 abalone (oyster) mushroom, or fresh field mushroom, finely sliced
1½in/4cm piece ginger, cut into matchstick pieces
2in/5cm piece pickled cabbage (Pak Gat Dong) or 3-4 pieces of pickled red cabbage, slivered lengthways
2in/5cm fresh red chilli, slivered lengthways
2 spring onions/scallions, finely sliced into 2in/5cm pieces
2 tbs/30ml fish sauce
1 tbs/15ml light soy sauce
½ tsp/2.5ml ground white pepper
1 tbs/15ml whisky (optional)
coriander leaves, to garnish

Put the prepared fish on a dish slightly larger than itself, which will fit into your steamer, or into a large saucepan with an inverted saucer or small bowl in the bottom of it. Place all the remaining ingredients, except the garnish on top of the fish. Put the dish in the steamer and steam for 20-25 minutes. Remove, garnish with the coriander and serve.

FRIED FISH WITH PORK, GINGER AND MUSHROOMS

Pla Jian

This is another simple dish and quite mild in flavour.

oil for deep frying, plus 2 tbs/30ml
1 pomfret or other small flat fish, cleaned, rinsed, and patted dry inside and out
2 garlic cloves, finely chopped
3oz/90g minced/ground pork
1 small carrot, cut diagonally into 4-5 pieces
1in/2.5cm piece ginger, finely slivered
4-6 pieces Thai dried black mushroom, soaked in water for about 15 minutes to soften
1 tsp/5ml yellow bean sauce
1 tbs/15ml light soy sauce
1 tbs/15ml fish sauce
1 tsp/5ml sugar
4 tbs/60 ml stock/broth
½ small onion, slivered
1 medium red chilli, finely slivered
2 spring onions/scallions, trimmed and coarsely chopped
generous shake of ground white pepper

Heat the oil and deep-fry the fish until golden brown and crisp. Remove, drain, place on a serving dish and set aside. While the fish is cooking, heat 2 tbs/30ml of oil in a wok or frying pan/skillet. Add the garlic and fry until golden brown. Add the pork, stir and cook until the meat is no longer pink. Add the remaining ingredients, one at a time, stirring and cooking for a second or two after each addition. Turn the mixture onto the cooked fish and serve.

THREE-FLAVOURED FISH

Pla Lat Prik

This dish typifies Thai cooking: it combines three opposing flavours – sweet, sour and hot – yet allows each to remain distinct and separate. This recipe also works well with sea bass but this is, unfortunately, extremely expensive. However, if you prefer to make this recipe with bass, buy a medium-sized fish and grill/broil rather than fry it.

1 mackerel or whiting (about 1 lb/450g), cleaned and gutted with head left on
oil for deep frying
lettuce, to garnish

Sauce:
2 tbs/30ml oil
6 shallots, finely chopped
1 large garlic clove, finely chopped
4 red chillies, 3in/7.5cm long, deseeded and finely chopped
2 tbs/30ml fish sauce
2 tbs/30ml sugar
2 tbs/30ml lemon juice
2 tbs/30ml stock

Fill a frying pan large enough to hold the fish with oil to a depth of 1 in/2.5cm. Heat the oil until a light haze appears. Add the fish and fry until the skin (and some of the flesh) is crisp and golden on both sides, making sure it doesn't stick to the pan.

While the fish is cooking, make the sauce. In a small frying pan heat 2 tbs/30ml oil and fry the shallots until crisp and brown, then remove with a slotted spoon and set aside. Fry the garlic until golden brown, remove with a slotted spoon, and set aside. Pour off most of the oil from the pan leaving a light film. Return half the cooked shallots and garlic to the pan and add the chillies, fish sauce, sugar, lemon juice and stock. Stir until the sugar is dissolved and the mixture starts to thicken slightly. Add the remaining shallots and garlic, stir and remove from heat.

Arrange the lettuce on a serving dish. When the fish is cooked, remove from the pan and place on the bed of lettuce. Pour the sauce over and serve.

Above: Sun-drying squid at Rayong. Left: Opening giant Thai oysters

BABY CLAMS IN BATTER WITH EGG AND CHILLI

Hoy Tohd

Batter:
3 tbs/45ml rice flour
3 tbs/45ml wheat flour
2 eggs
pinch of salt
8fl oz/240ml/1cup water
1½lbs baby clams, shelled
(should yield 4-6oz/120-180g meat)
3 tbs/45ml oil, plus extra if necessary
1 garlic clove, finely chopped
ground white pepper
1 tbs/15ml light soy sauce
2 tbs/30ml fish sauce
1 tsp/5ml sugar
handful beansprouts
1 spring onion/scallion, coarsely chopped
coriander leaf for garnish
Sauce:
3 tbs/45ml rice vinegar
2 small chillies, sliced into fine rings
½ tsp/2.5ml sugar

Put the flours in a basin and mix thoroughly with the pinch of salt. Break one egg into the flour mixture, mix, add the water. Whisk thoroughly together, making sure there are no lumps; the mixture should have the consistency of thick cream. Add the shelled clams and set aside.

In a large frying pan/skillet, heat the oil and fry the garlic until golden. Add the clam and batter mixture, tipping the pan to spread it evenly over the surface to form a pancake. Turn after 1-2 minutes (it will cook quickly), and cook the other side briefly. With a spatula and wooden spoon, or similar instruments, quickly tear the clam pancake into five or six pieces. Lower the heat and break the second egg into the pan. Quickly cook the pancake pieces in the egg. Add a little more oil if necessary, and then a sprinkling of white pepper, the soy sauce, fish sauce and sugar, turning the pancake pieces quickly as you work. Add the beansprouts and spring onion and turn together quickly. Turn the mixture onto a heated dish and garnish with coriander. In a small bowl, blend the vinegar, chillies and sugar and serve with the clam cake.

Hauling in the nets at dusk on Lamai beach on the island of Koh Samui

HOT AND SOUR SEAFOOD SALAD
Yam Talay

This is only for lovers of chilli. It has a very sharp, lemony taste and is often served as a pre-meal starter with drinks: its electric flavour is said to sober up those who've had one too many. It can be made with any combination of seafood.

lettuce, parsley, cucumber, etc. to garnish
2 tbs/30ml lemon juice
1 tsp/5ml chilli powder
2 tbs/30ml stock/broth
1 tsp/5ml sugar
2 tbs/30ml fish sauce
4 prepared fish balls (from an oriental store)
4 large raw prawns, shelled and deveined
2-4 crab claws
4 pieces sliced squid
2 lime leaves, finely sliced
1 shallot, finely chopped
½ small onion, finely slivered
sprig of coriander leaf, coarsely chopped

Prepare a serving dish with lettuce, parsley and sliced cucumber and set aside. Combine the lemon juice, chilli powder, stock, sugar and fish sauce in a small pan. Bring to the boil, stirring all the time. Add the fish balls, prawns, crab claws and squid, and stir and cook for a minute or two until the raw meats are cooked through. Take off the heat and add all the remaining ingredients. Mix well, turn onto the prepared dish, and serve.

PRAWNS WITH LEMON GRASS
Pla Gung

lettuce and parsley sprigs, to decorate
2 tbs/30ml lemon juice
2 tbs/30ml fish sauce
½ tsp/2.5ml chilli powder
1 tsp/5ml sugar
2 tbs/30ml stock/broth
4-6 large prawns, shelled and deveined
1 lime leaf, finely sliced
1 shallot, coarsely chopped
⅓ lemon grass stalk, finely chopped
½ small onion, slivered
1 spring onion/scallion, cut into 1in/2.5cm pieces

Prepare a small serving plate with lettuce and sprigs of parsley.

Boil the lemon juice with the fish sauce, chilli powder, sugar and stock for about a minute in a small pan, over high heat, stirring. Add the shelled prawns and cook quickly until the prawns are opaque. The liquid should be considerably reduced. Add the remaining ingredients, stir once, remove from the heat and transfer immediately to the prepared plate.

leaves), stirring and cooking for a few seconds after each addition. Turn onto the prepared serving dish and garnish with the coriander leaves.

STEAMED CRAB MEAT
Bu Ja

The first time you make this recipe you will need to buy 4 crab shells as well as the meat, the next time you can just buy the crab meat. If crab shells are unavailable, use heatproof ramekins instead.

3 garlic cloves
3 coriander roots
4oz/120g crabmeat
4oz/120g minced/ground pork
1 egg
2 tbs/30ml fish sauce
1 tbs/15ml light soy sauce
½ tsp/2.5ml sugar
4 crab shells
Garnish:
8 fine slivers red chilli (or red pepper)
8 fine slivers green chilli (or green pepper)
8 coriander leaves

Pound the garlic with the coriander roots. Mix all the ingredients, except the garnishes, thoroughly together. Put the mixture into the crab shells (or ramekins) and arrange in a steamer. Steam for 15 minutes. Remove and garnish with the slivers of green and red chilli and coriander leaves.

STEAMED CRAB CLAWS
Bu Op

This dish is traditionally cooked in a clay pot which can be bought in most Chinese or oriental stores.

2 tbs/30ml oil
2 garlic cloves, finely chopped
3oz/90g dry *Wun Sen* noodles (p. 86), soaked for 15 minutes in cold water and drained
1in/2.5cm piece ginger, cut into matchstick strips
2 celery stalks/sticks, sliced diagonally
2oz/60g broccoli florets
2oz/60g spring greens/cabbage, coarsely chopped
4-6 crab claws, depending on size
1 tsp/5ml dark soy sauce
1 tbs/15ml light soy sauce
½ tsp/2.5ml sugar
2 tbs/30ml fish sauce
1 tbs/15ml oyster sauce
2 tbs/30ml stock/broth or water

In a wok or large frying pan, heat the oil, add the garlic and fry until golden brown. Add the vermicelli, stir quickly, then add the ginger, celery, broccoli and cabbage and stir briefly. Add the crab claws and stir. Add all the remaining ingredients, stir quickly, cover and steam gently for 3-4 minutes. If you think the mixture is becoming too dry, add a little more stock or water.

SQUID WITH VEGETABLES AND OYSTER SAUCE
Plamuk Patpak Namanhoy

This is another variation of a basic Thai theme: meat or fish plus crisp fresh vegetables. In this case it's squid with whatever seasonal vegetables are available; I have suggested ingredients that look good (a very Thai way of approaching food), but the really important thing is to use whatever vegetables are freshest when you shop.

6oz/180g squid (bodies only), rinsed and drained if bought ready prepared
2 tbs/30ml oil
2 garlic cloves, finely chopped
1 tbs/15ml oyster sauce
4-5 small baby corn, each cut lengthwise into 2-3 pieces
2 tbs/30ml fish sauce
1 tbs/15ml light soy sauce
½ tsp/2.5ml sugar
1 large red chilli, sliced into rings
about 2 tbs/30 ml water
4-5 pieces dried mushroom, soaked in water for 15 minutes and sliced if necessary
10 stalks Thai spring flower (available from specialist stores) or 2 spring onions/scallions, cut into 1½-2in/4-5cm pieces
5-6 mangetout/snow peas, trimmed
5-6 small broccoli florets

Slice the squid bodies into rings and set aside. In a wok or large frying pan, heat the oil, add the garlic and fry until golden brown. Add the oyster sauce and baby corn and stir. Then add the squid, stir and cook for a few seconds. Add the remaining ingredients, one at a time, stirring after each addition. Cook briefly until the broccoli is a good bright green and still crisp, and the squid is cooked through, opaque, and slightly shrunken. If you feel the mixture is becoming too dry, add a little more water.

SQUID WITH DRY CURRY
Plamuk Patpet

This dish is hot. Its appeal lies in the contrast between the bland squid and green aubergines/eggplant, and the fiery attack of the red chillies.

6-8oz/180-230g squid (bodies only), washed and cleaned
3 tbs/45ml oil
2 garlic cloves, finely chopped
2 tsp/10ml Red curry paste (p. 93)
2 tbs/30ml fish sauce
1 tbs/15ml light soy sauce
1 tsp/5ml sugar
2-3 small green aubergine/eggplant, quartered, or Western aubergine
1 small red chilli, finely chopped
2 lime leaves, finely sliced
10 leaves holy basil

Score the squid quite finely on both sides, and cut into pieces, about 1 in/2.5cm square. In a wok or frying pan, over medium-high flame, heat the oil, add the garlic and fry until golden brown. Add the curry paste, mix, and cook for a few seconds. Now add the squid, mix and cook briefly. Stirring all the time, add the remaining ingredients, pausing after the addition of the aubergines to give them a few seconds to cook. When the squid is cooked through and opaque, give a final stir, pour the mixture onto a warmed dish and serve.

Sorting fresh green-tinged mussels, like the oysters, much larger than in the West

STUFFED SQUID SOUP
Gang Juhd Pla Muk Yat Sai

4oz/120g minced/ground pork
2 garlic cloves, finely chopped
½ tsp/2.5ml ground white pepper
1 tbs/15ml fish sauce
½ tsp/2.5 ml sugar
5-6 small squid body sacs (3-4in/8-10cm long)
1pt/570ml stock/broth
2 tbs/30ml fish sauce
2 tbs/30ml light soy sauce
1 tsp/5ml preserved radish (*tang chi*, p. 39)
½ tsp/2.5ml ground white pepper
2 spring onions/scallions, cut into 1in/2.5cm pieces

Thoroughly combine the pork, garlic, white pepper, 1 tbs fish sauce and sugar. Stuff the mixture into the squid sacs, taking care not to overfill them since the filling will swell in cooking. In a medium-sized pan, heat the stock and add 2 tbs fish sauce, soy sauce, preserved radish, and pepper. When thoroughly blended and heated through, bring to a simmer, add the stuffed squid and cook gently for 4-5 minutes. The squid will shrink and the meat mixture cook through. Add the sliced spring onions and serve in small bowls.

STEAMED MUSSELS WITH LEMON GRASS & BASIL
Hoy Op

Those used to cooking mussels with cream and wine will be pleasantly surprised by the simplicity of this Thai recipe. Galangal, lemon grass and holy basil all delicately enhance the mussel flavour.

1-1½lb/450-700g mussels, cleaned, debearded, and rinsed
3in/8cm piece galangal, in 3-4 pieces
2 lemon grass stalks, cut into 3in/8cm pieces and lightly crushed
10 sprigs holy basil
Sauce:
1 large garlic clove, finely chopped
1 tsp/5ml chopped chilli
2 tbs/30ml lemon juice
1 tbs/15ml light soy sauce
2 tbs/30ml fish sauce
1 tsp/5ml sugar

Place the mussels, galangal, lemon grass and basil in a large saucepan. Add enough water to come ½ in/1cm up the pan. Cover, place over medium heat and steam for about 15 minutes or until the mussels have opened. Discard any mussels that do not open.

Combine the sauce ingredients in a small bowl. Serve the mussels in a large bowl, with the sauce nearby for dipping the mussels into.

BABY CLAMS WITH BLACK BEAN SAUCE

Hoy Pat Tow Jeow

This dish is best made with small sweet clams, rather than with the big clams that are most usual in North American cooking.

2 tbs/30ml oil
2 garlic cloves, finely chopped
1 lb/450g baby clams in the shell
2 tbs/30ml light soy sauce
1 small red chilli, finely chopped
1 tsp/5ml black bean sauce
4 tbs/60ml water
10 leaves holy basil

In a wok or large frying pan, heat the oil, add the garlic and fry until golden brown. Add the baby clams and stir thoroughly. Add the soy sauce, chilli, black bean sauce, and the water. Stir thoroughly, add the basil, cover the pan and leave to steam for a few minutes until the clams have opened. Discard any that have not opened. Stir again, turn onto a warmed dish and serve.

STEAMED SCALLOPS WITH GARLIC

Hoy Nung Kratiem Jeow

A delicate starter, easy to make, but very luxurious.

6 scallops on the shell, cleaned
3 tbs/45ml oil
3 garlic cloves, finely chopped
1 small red or green chilli, sliced into fine rings
Sauce:
3 tbs/45ml light soy sauce
1in/2.5cm piece ginger, finely chopped
1 tsp/5ml sugar
1 small red chilli, finely chopped
Garnish:
2 tbs/30ml spring onion/scallion, sliced into fine rings
6 coriander leaves

Set the scallops on their shells in a steamer over 1-2 in/2.5-5cm hot water. In a small frying pan, heat the oil, add the garlic and fry until golden brown. Pour a spoonful of garlic and oil over each scallop, add a little sliced chilli, cover, and steam over medium heat until the scallops are cooked (10-15 minutes). While the scallops steam, mix together all the sauce ingredients.

When the scallops are cooked, remove from the steamer, place on a serving dish and garnish with the spring onion and coriander leaves. Serve the sauce on the side.

CRAB OMELETTE

Kai Jeow Poo

3oz/90g white crabmeat
1 tsp/5ml sesame oil
1 tbs/15ml white wine
3 eggs
2 tbs/15ml coconut cream
½ tsp/2.5ml salt
shaking of ground white pepper
1 tbs/15ml finely slivered ginger
1 tbs/15ml finely slivered carrot
1 tbs/15ml finely slivered onion
1 tbs/15ml finely slivered bamboo shoot
1 tbs/15ml finely sliced straw mushrooms
2 tbs/30ml oil
coriander leaves, to garnish

Combine the crabmeat, sesame oil and white wine in a small bowl and set aside. In a bowl, lightly beat the eggs with the coconut cream, salt and pepper. Add the crab mixture and blend lightly. Add the ginger, carrot, onion, bamboo shoot and mushrooms. Lightly mix together.

In a wok or frying pan, heat the oil until a light haze appears. Pour the mixture into the oil. With a spatula, gently lift the egg from the sides of the wok as it cooks to allow the uncooked mixture to set. Turn it over, and cook for a few seconds. When the omelette is set, slide it onto a serving dish and garnish with coriander leaves.

UP COUNTRY

FOOD FROM THE NORTHERN REGIONS
OF THAILAND

s the morning mist clears across a heavily wooded valley a young man is picking wild mushrooms by a stream, laying them carefully in a chipped enamel bowl. These mushrooms are quite unlike the neat button variety eaten in Europe. They look more like undulant sea creatures the colour of old ivory. These meaty fungi will provide a tasty part of the morning meal and they are free, which is no bad thing. Walking back to his hamlet, the man seems, at a distance, to be passing through untamed forest but close-to can be seen patches of cultivation between the trees where rice and vegetables are growing. These are the foothills of the mountain range that rises into the Golden Triangle, the high northern region that Thailand shares with Burma and Laos. Beyond this valley live the hill tribes who are racially different from the lowland Thai. In the extreme northern highlands, these tribes are often a law unto themselves. Locked in their mountain strongholds War Lords control the opium trade, slipping across the frontiers to escape the Thai army.

King Rama VII entering Chiang Mai on an elephant, 1927

But all that is far away. Here, safe beside the regional capital, Chiang Mai, a new day breaks clear at Wat Chet Yot unveiling the ancient carvings on its tall square Chedi. Even a short-term visitor coming from Bangkok will see that this temple is different in style from those in the south. The Chedi, with its seven spires, is decorated with bas-relief figures, princely in appearance, whose elegant limbs are turned as if in some formal dance, their lips frozen in serene smiles. The design of this temple, like many in the north has been heavily influenced by neighbouring Burma. Wat Chet Yot is one of the most famous centres in Buddhist history as it was here, in 1477, that the king of then independent Chiang Mai, Tilokaraje, summoned a great Council from all over Asia to re-vise the sacred teachings of the Buddha. The temple itself is a copy of that in Pagan, Burma, which itself was copied from that in Bodh Gaya, India where the Buddha achieved enlighten-ment. Inside the vaulted prayer-hall the huge wooden Buddha has the almost doll-like simplicity that we associate with Bur-mese folk art, a distinct contrast to the refined carvings on the outside walls. The temple tells us much about the north and its remoteness from the centre of Thai culture. The influence of Burma has filtered into the art, the customs, and of course the food of Chiang Mai. This northern city is the Bankokians favourite escape from the hot season humidity of the capital and whereas the southerners delight in telling rude jokes about the ignorance of provincials, especially the peoples of the

Page 124: A Burmese-style temple nestling in the foot-hills of Northern Thailand

north east whose accent is considered amusing, they have nothing but praise for the citizens of Chiang Mai, who are said to
be more polite, more generous and helpful. They also say that
the girls of Chiang Mai are the prettiest in the country and that
the region's food is the tastiest.

Some years back, my aunt and uncle bought part of Mae Sae
valley, in the hills to the north west of the town, and created a
garden resort with pleasant flowerbeds on slopes running
down to a river at the valley bottom. Among these plants and
shrubs are thatched cottages where tired city folk can spend a
relaxing weekend. Like me, my aunt was a student in Britain
and is passionate about the English garden so that foreign
visitors are sometimes puzzled when they find themselves ad-
miring well-tended borders of geraniums, or whatever bulbs

*Ancient stucco on
the wall of Wat Chet
Yot on the outskirts
of Chiang Mai*

Mr Gee and his family enjoy a meal they have grown and cooked themselves

she has brought back from her holidays or that I have been prevailed upon to send her. And not just flowers, my aunt experiments with all sorts of temperate plants and her kitchen gardens now supply the big Bangkok hotels with rare Italian salads and French vegetables. Of course, this is all part of an honourable Thai tradition of drawing new elements into our cuisine – the Portuguese introduced the chilli which they brought from the Americas in the seventeenth century, and more recently we have added the tomato, the potato, carrots, celery and sweet peppers. It is a living tradition. The formal English garden is much admired by the Thai, who greatly envy the open spaces of English cities. At Mae Sae valley there is a chance to enjoy that pleasure in the cool clear highland air. Today, most visitors fly up but for the full effect you should take the old fashioned train which chugs its way overnight up the length of the country, crossing the wide rice paddies of the central plains and passing on to the vast teak forests of the north.

In among those forests, near my family's resort, the traditional life of the north goes on. Returning with his bowl of mushrooms, our young man greets his father-in-law at work in his patch of rice. They cultivate sticky, or glutinous rice, the staple food of the region. Sticky rice is only a novelty in the rest of the world, and even in Bangkok we seldom eat it except as a dessert, so it has little export value and the farmers here its popularity grew, so did Ba Yon's work. A daughter-in-law tried to open a rival business in Bangkok, to supply the city's supermarkets, but people only wanted the sausage if it bore the name of Ba Yon. To help her family she let the younger woman use her recipe and her name. In Chiang Mai, the original business is still a relatively domestic affair carried out on the ground floor of her home even though much of the grinding and mixing is now done by modern machinery. Hygenic cellophane wrappers have recently been introduced though these are ultimately wrapped in banana leaves for tradition's sake. But even with these new concessions to health, Ba Yon still advises customers to eat the sausage after three days, though her daughter told me that there are certain daredevil gourmets who relish the taste after five days, and are willing to accept the risks involved in satisfying their craving.

Ba Yon's 'raw' sausage is only one of many varieties of Chiang Mai charcuterie. Most are cooked and you can see them grilling and frying on stalls in the Wararot food market near the city's main klong. The smells are delicious. A walk round Wararot reveals the abundance of northern produce and may explain why this of all the Thai regions has not been part of the great drain from the countryside to the capital. Chiang Mai has much to offer its people, but sadly the neighbouring north east has no such bounty. Unlike Chiang Mai with its plentiful rains, the north east has known little but drought in recent years with the result that the Issan peoples of the region have become the country's migrant workers. Many of the fishermen at Hua Hin are today from that once remote area, and how they take to a life on board ship when they come from so far away from the sea I cannot imagine. At the end of our *soi* in Bangkok there is an Issan woman who grills marinated chicken in the characteristic Issan fashion: splayed and gripped in a bamboo fork. No doubt she travelled by crowded bus down the dusty silver Friendship Highway, built by the Americans to service their bases near our border on the Mekong River, during the Vietnam War. To take that route is to pass beyond the ordered world of tourist coaches and international hotels, but there is still much to discover. At Ban Chiang you can see evidence in the form of unique and beautiful pottery of a civilization between 7,000 and 8,000 years old that has only recently been identified. Ban Chiang may be the world's oldest culture. Near the eastern city of Korat is Pimai, in the twelfth century the most westerly outpost of Angkor Wat, the great Khmer temple in Cambodia. Pimai's cave-like galleries have a mysterious air so different from the colourful openness of a Thai temple

Despite the poverty of the region, its people, like all Thais, know how to relax. When I was last in Korat there was a festival in progress and that night everyone gathered at the local sports ground to enjoy the foodstalls, amusement arcades, side-shows and open-air cinema. A favourite attraction was the one-baht dance where in exchange for that small coin the local lads could have a minute's dance with one of the mini-skirted girls provided by the management. Oddly enough, the boys were usually so concerned to show their dancing technique to their watching friends they barely noticed the young ladies swaying along beside them. Sadly, many of these young people will be forced to leave Korat to try to make their way in the big city. It is at this point that the radio and television soap operas have become all too real, the universal struggle of country people to survive in the strange metropolis. One hopeful sign is that the government has recently announced long-term plans to improve agriculture in these once forgotten regions. The leader in these moves has always been our present King, who has made a special point of interesting himself in irrigation schemes. In the grounds of his home in Bangkok, the Chitrilada Palace, he maintains an experimental farm that investigates new dairy processes and tries out new varieties of seeds and plants. His Majesty and his consort Queen Sirikit have taken a special interest in the hill tribes to the north of Chiang Mai, trying to persuade them to adopt crops other than opium. It is a slow, often disappointing process, but one that has to go on if the trade in human misery is to be wiped out. The Queen has done much to promote northern handicrafts as a way of bringing much needed cash into the region. That, and the growth of tourism, should give the peoples of the north some alternative to the production of drugs.

Of course, only the hardiest visitors, willing to go hill trekking, will really see the hill tribes in their remote villages. There are six main groups: Karen, Hmong, Mien, Lahu, Akha and Lisu, and while each has its own language, history and culture, they all share a love of richly-embroidered costumes in vivid colours, often red and black, and love to see their womenfolk weighed down with massive silver ornaments.

The less adventurous can get some idea of mountain life at the various folk spectacles now laid on for visitors to Chiang Mai and while these are inevitably a mere shadow of the

Hill tribes in the North, a group of Akha *women and girls in traditional dress*

1 lb/450g minced/ground pork (about 15% fat)
2 stalks lemon grass, finely chopped
5 coriander roots, finely chopped
10 lime leaves, finely chopped
2 large garlic cloves, finely chopped
4 shallots, finely chopped
1in/2.5cm piece galangal, finely chopped
2 tbs/30ml Red curry paste (p. 93)
1 tsp/5ml powdered turmeric
½ tsp/2.5ml salt
1 tbs/15ml fish sauce
3 tbs/45ml cooked rice
oil for deep frying

Mix all the ingredients thoroughly together. With the aid of a funnel or a large icing nozzle, force the mixture into the sausage skin, leaving a 2 in/5cm length of unfilled skin in between each 6-8 in/15-20cm of sausage. Try to ensure that the diameter of each sausage is not less than 1 in/2.5cm. Cut in between the sausages to separate them, and knot the unfilled skin at each end of the sausage to make sure the filling won't escape during cooking.

When the sausages are ready, prick them with a fork. Heat oil in deep fryer to medium heat (if the oil is too hot, the sausages are likely to burst). Fry the sausages for 5-6 minutes until well-browned. Remove from oil and drain. Slice diagonally and serve.

SOUR GARLIC SAUSAGE
Si Graw Priow

Ask your butcher for pork intestine to use as sausage casings.

6oz/180g minced/ground pork (about 15% fat)
2oz/60g cooked rice, plain or sticky
2 garlic cloves, finely chopped
¼ tsp/1.25ml salt
½ tsp/2.5ml ground white pepper
Salad:
lettuce
1in/2.5cm piece ginger, finely slivered
3 spring onions/scallions, finely slivered
handful parsley, coarsely chopped
handful coriander leaves, coarsely chopped
1 small red chilli, finely slivered

Thoroughly mix the pork, rice, garlic, salt and pepper. Using a funnel or large icing nozzle, force the mixture into the sausage skin, tying

off each sausage at 1½-2 in/4-5cm lengths. You should have 6-8 small sausages. Cover and leave overnight in a dry warm place (in a cooling oven, or near a radiator; in Thailand they would be left in the sun to dry out partially).

They may be cooked the following day, or stored in the refrigerator for 2-3 days. When you are ready to cook them, prick them with a fork and fry or grill/broil. Combine the salad ingredients and serve with the sausages.

SKEWERED MARINATED PORK
Moo Ping

This makes about 12 skewers, and will serve 4-6 people.

Skewers:
2 garlic cloves, finely chopped
6 coriander roots, finely chopped
4 tbs/60ml fish sauce
1 tbs/15ml light soy sauce
4fl oz/125ml/½ cup thick coconut cream
4fl oz/125ml/½cup oil
1 tbs/15ml sugar
½ tsp/2.5ml ground white pepper
1 lb/450g lean pork, thinly sliced into
1½ × 3in/4 × 7.5cm pieces
Sauce:
1 tbs/15ml fish sauce
2 tbs/30ml lemon juice
1 tbs/15ml light soy sauce
1 tsp/5ml chilli powder
1 tbs/15ml sugar
1 tbs/15ml coarsely chopped coriander

Combine all the skewer ingredients, except the pork, until thoroughly blended. Add the pork and mix in, making sure that each piece is thoroughly coated. Let stand for at least 30 minutes; longer if possible. While the meat is marinating, place all the sauce ingredients in a small bowl and mix well. Taste; if too hot, add more fish sauce, lemon juice and sugar.

Pre-heat the grill/broiler. Take 12 × 6-8in/ 15-20cm wooden skewers and thread 2 pieces of meat on each, making sure that as much of the surface of the meat as possible will be exposed to the grill. (Make more skewers if you have meat left over.) Grill/broil over a high heat for 2-3 minutes each side, or until the meat is thoroughly cooked through. Serve on a dish garnished with lettuce, parsley or coriander, with the sauce on the side.

CHILLI SOUP
Gaeng Prik

This is a marvellously spicy soup, made even more so with the addition of the optional chilli powder.

10 small dried chillies
2 garlic cloves, chopped
1in/2.5cm piece galangal, chopped
2 shallots, chopped
½ stalk lemon grass, chopped
1 tsp/5ml shrimp paste
¼ tsp/1.5ml ground white pepper
2 pt/1 litre/5 cups stock/broth
4oz/120g lean pork, cut into fine strips
4 tbs/60ml fish sauce
½ tsp/2.5ml sugar
½ tsp/2.5ml chilli powder (optional)
1 tbs/15ml chopped spring onion/scallion
1 tbs/15ml chopped coriander leaf
Serves 6

Using a pestle and mortar or blender, pound or blend the chillies, garlic, galangal, shallots, lemon grass, shrimp paste and pepper together to make a paste. In a large saucepan, bring the stock to the boil. Add 1 tbs/15ml of the pounded mixture and stir to mix well. Add the pieces of pork and bring back to the boil. Skim if necessary. Add the fish sauce, sugar, and chilli powder if you wish. Stir quickly to mix thoroughly. Reduce the heat and simmer for a minute. The meat should be completely cooked through. Pour the soup into a tureen, garnish with the spring onion and coriander and serve.

CHIANG MAI CURRY NOODLE
Kow Soi

4oz/120g fresh *Ba Mee* noodles (p. 86), or use 2oz/60g dry noodles soaked in water for 15 minutes, and drained
2 tbs/30ml oil
1 small garlic clove, finely chopped
1 tsp/5ml Red curry paste (p. 93)
4fl oz/125ml/½cup thick coconut milk
4oz/120g minced/ground pork
½pt/250ml stock/broth
1 tsp/5ml curry powder
¼ tsp/1.5ml turmeric powder
2 tbs/30ml fish sauce
½ tsp/2.5ml sugar
½ tsp/2.5ml lemon juice

To garnish:
1 spring onion/scallion, coarsely chopped
2 shallots, finely diced
1 tbs/15ml pickled cabbage (Gat Pak Dong)
1 lemon, cut into wedges

Bring a pan of water to the boil, and, using a sieve or mesh strainer, dip the noodles into the water for a few seconds. Drain and set aside in a serving bowl. In a wok or frying pan/skillet, heat the oil, add the garlic and fry quickly until golden. Add the curry paste, mix in, and cook for a few seconds. Add the coconut milk, mix in and cook until the liquid starts to reduce. Add the pork and stir thoroughly, then add the stock, curry powder, turmeric, fish sauce, sugar and lemon juice, stirring after each addition. By this time the pork should be cooked through. Cook over a high heat, stirring constantly, for about 10 seconds. Pour the mixture over the noodles, garnish and serve.

SLICED STEAK WITH HOT AND SOUR SAUCE
Nua Yang

lettuce, carrot and cucumber, to garnish
6oz/180g lean steak
1 tbs/15ml lemon juice
1 tbs/15ml fish sauce
1 tsp/5ml sugar
1 tsp/5ml chilli powder
2 shallots, finely sliced
1 small spring onion/scallion, chopped
1 sprig coriander leaf, coarsely chopped

Arrange the lettuce, carrot and cucumber on a serving plate.

Pre-heat the grill/broiler. When really hot, grill/broil the steak so that the meat remains rare on the inside. Slice thinly and set aside. In a bowl, mix together the lemon juice, fish sauce, sugar and chilli powder. Add the shallots, spring onions and the reserved beef. Stir quickly, turn onto the serving dish and sprinkle the coriander leaf over.

Siam into a modern nation. Sadly, this noble man had the misfortune to hire an English governess, Anna Leonowens, to teach the royal princes. It is not known if he ever met her, for she had hardly arrived at the palace before home sickness drove her back to England. Short of money, she wrote a fanciful account of the 'exotic' court of which she claimed to have been a privileged member and this has come down to us as *The King and I*. The real King Mongkut was a saintly man who spent much of his life as a monk, but Yul Brynner's portrayal is probably the only image most people have of my country. Not that we are unduly upset by the film; though it is banned in Thailand out of respect for the King's memory, almost every Thai who travels abroad has seen it and enjoyed it as a piece of fiction which has as much to do with our country as a film about the planet Mars.

The real Siam can be found not far from King Mongkut's palace on the outskirts of Phetchaburi, after a fairly long walk up a steep tree-lined slope to the Khao Luang Cave. In the cavernous interior are huge stalactites eerily lit by a shaft of

The statue of the Emerald Buddha, the most sacred shrine in Thailand

Intricately carved fruits: crab apple, papaya, rose apple and water melon transformed into flowers

natural light. We Thais look on caves as ready-made temples and fill them with Buddha images and this particular cavern has many, glistening in the half-light. Phetchaburi also has a marvellous man-made temple complex, part of which predates the founding of Bangkok and so gives some idea of the glories of Thai art and architecture before the Burmese destroyed Ayuthaya in the eighteenth century. The façades of Wat Mahathat are covered with intricately carved stucco work like some fabulous oriental wedding cake, but the interior of the ordination hall glows with murals of Thai life, wonderfully detailed paintings that are presently threatened by the destructive effects of damp and are in urgent need of restoration.

Most of the great occasions in Thai life, whether personal or national, have a religious element. Before the establishment of the European Sunday, we had a continuous working week broken up by many Temple holy days usually ordained by the lunar calendar. Today we have a five- or six-day working week with a number of national holidays, half religious, half royal or patriotic, though even they usually involve some sort of Buddhist rite. April the sixth, for example, is Chakri Day when we celebrate the founding of the present dynasty and people in Bangkok try to take flowers and incense to the Temple of the Emerald Buddha and then visit the nearby Pantheon of Royal Statues which is opened only on that one day. The King is the focus of many holidays. His Majesty's birthday, the anniversary of his coronation and the Queen's birthday are all National Holidays celebrated with parades and fireworks. It is during these great national events when the King hosts a reception or a banquet that Thai food is seen in its most exalted form with incredible attention played to the beauty of presentation. This means not only that the food should be stylishly set out on fine dishes but that it is also decorated with exquisitely carved fruit and vegetables. All Thai cooks decorate their food, though on an everyday basis this usually means little more than gar-

Look Choob:
*deceptive sweets
moulded to look like
tiny vegetables*

becomes a monk for a short period and when someone in the
family marries. Nearly all Thai males enter a monastery at
some time, even the present King did so as a young man. When
I became a monk in 1973 my family invited relatives and
friends to celebrate on the day before I entered the monastery
and on the day itself food was taken to the temple as a gift for
the monks. On arrival my parents symbolically clipped my hair
before one of the monks shaved my head and a period of
abstinence began in which I begged for my food and ate the
final meal of the day at the end of the morning. In Bangkok the
food offered to visitors on this occasion is relatively modest
compared to the lavish feasting in the countryside. I once
visited the village of Si Satchenali in the centre of Thailand to
see the celebrations when the boys entered the monastery and
was overwhelmed at the scale of the ceremony. On the
previous day, every woman in the village was cooking; great
vats of rice were being boiled up under the stilt houses; and
every home was willingly offering its best to any visitor who
cared to call. The next day, the boys were shaved and
sumptuously dressed, and each had his own elephant to carry
him in a great procession round the village accompanied by
anyone who could move, or rather, dance. It was a spectacle
out of the past that slowly wound its way to the temple.

The one occasion when the capital rivals the countryside is a
wedding. Still in Thailand, the union of a man and a woman
really means the union of two families and the setting up of a
complex set of relationships very important in a culture where
families are still expected to help each other a great deal. Thus
a wedding is a major public statement. My youngest brother
Ooie's wedding was the most recent in my immediate family
and although it was not on the scale of the great social
weddings made among the big business families that we read
about in newspapers, it lacked nothing in terms of cramming as
many occasions to eat and drink as possible into twenty-four
hours. We began in the morning when my family accompanied

Ooie from our house to his fiancée's home, each of us bearing gifts of sweetmeats, flowers and presents. Both families were now formally introduced to each other and the young couple paid their respects to the oldest members of both groups. Throughout, there was a constant flow of delicacies for everyone. After about an hour an official came from the town hall to complete the civil formalities and then a group of monks from a nearby temple came to bless the union and accept food. At the end of the morning we took our brother back home, for although he was legally married, the true marriage occurs only when the bride is formally brought back to our house, and that would be later. That afternoon, the arrangements were a mix of a traditional Thai and a modern Western marriage. Relatives and friends were invited to one of the main luxury hotels where two large reception rooms had been booked. Ooie wore his dress uniform as a newly qualified police officer and Aw, his wife, wore the full length white dress of a European wedding. After standing on line to receive members of the immediate family, they moved to a raised dais at the end of the first room where they knelt at prayer stools so that all could pass and sprinkle lustral water on their hands and wish them well. After that, everyone moved to the adjoining room to which friends and colleagues had been invited, and a full-blown reception with food, drink, toasts, speeches, and cake-cutting took place. As I have said elsewhere, traditionally we did not have hors d'oeuvres or snacks or cocktail food as such, rather the earliest cooked dishes were brought out to be 'tasted' with drinks. Now, however, we have adopted the habit of having something small to nibble before the meal proper begins or as 'finger-food' for parties, and a whole range of Thai appetizers has been developed.

Weddings are also occasions to serve the most refined of Thai sweets, Look Choob, which were once served only to the Kings of Siam and their court. They are so delicate and difficult to make that nowadays there are few left who are skilled at the task. The word 'look' can mean fruit and 'choob' means to dip, and to make Look Choob you mix a paste of soya beans, sugar and coconut juice that tastes like marzipan and fashion it into deceptive miniature replicas of fruit and vegetables, tiny bright red chillies, little baby eggplant, cherries and grapes, which are then coloured and dipped in clear gelatin to provide a waxy glaze, so that at a glance it is impossible to realize that they are not real. The fun lies in popping a whole 'chilli' into your mouth yet eating something deliciously sweet. Look Choob are still served on Royal occasions but ordinary folk like to have them for their wedding receptions even though they are very expensive.

After my brother's reception our family took the newly-weds to our home with members of the bride's family as guests, and supper was served – a thick soup of polished rice to complete the day's eating. Then the longest married couple in our family went to the newly decorated bedroom and lay on the marriage

SWEETCORN CAKE
Tod Man Khao Pohd

12 oz/340g sweetcorn (canned or frozen: if using canned, drain well)
1 tbs/15ml curry powder
2 tbs/30ml rice flour
3 tbs/45ml wheat flour
½ tsp/2.5ml salt
2 tbs/30ml light soy sauce
oil for deep frying
Sauce:
4 tbs/60ml rice vinegar
2 tbs/30ml sugar
1in/2.5cm piece cucumber, quartered lengthwise, then finely sliced
½ small carrot, halved lengthwise, then finely sliced
2 shallots, finely sliced
1 tbs/15ml ground roasted peanuts
1 small red or green chilli, finely sliced

Mix all the ingredients (except the oil) together. Heat the oil in a deep-fryer. Using a tablespoon, take a spoonful of the mixture at a time, compressing each one slightly with the fingers to make a small cake, and slide into the hot oil. Fry until deep golden brown. Remove the cakes with a slotted spoon and drain.

Make the sauce. Boil the vinegar and sugar together in a small pan, stirring constantly, until the sugar dissolves and the mixture begins to thicken slightly. Remove from heat and allow to cool. Pour into a small bowl, add the remaining ingredients and stir to mix. Serve with the cakes.

CHICKEN SATAY
Satay

Satay is now as universal as the hamburger. Malaysian satay was originally introduced into our cuisine via our southern, Muslim region. These satays can also be made with pork or beef.

1 tsp/5ml coriander seeds
1 tsp/5ml cumin seeds
3 chicken breasts
2 tbs/30ml light soy sauce
1 tsp/5ml salt
4 tbs/60ml oil
1 tbs/15ml curry powder
1 tbs/15ml ground turmeric
8 tbs/120ml coconut milk
3 tbs/45ml sugar

Roast the coriander and cumin seeds gently in a small frying pan without oil for about 5 minutes, stirring and shaking to ensure they don't burn. Remove from the heat and grind together to make a fine powder. (You could substitute ready-ground seeds if more convenient.)

With a sharp knife, cut the chicken breasts into fine slices (3in/7.5cm long × 1½in/4cm wide × ¼in/5mm thick). Put the slices in a bowl and add all the remaining ingredients, including the ground coriander and cumin. Mix thoroughly and stand overnight, or for 8 hours (you can prepare in the morning for the evening's meal).

Pre-heat the grill/broiler (we would normally use a charcoal or barbecue grill). Using 7-8in/18-20cm wooden satay sticks, thread 2 pieces of the marinated meat on each stick – not straight through the meat, but rather as if you were gathering or smocking a piece of material. Grill/broil the satays until the meat is cooked through – about 6-8 minutes – turning to make sure they are browned on both sides. Serve with Peanut Sauce and Cucumber Pickle.

PEANUT SAUCE

2 tbs/30ml oil
3 garlic cloves, finely chopped
1 tbs/15ml Massaman (p. 93) or Red curry paste (p. 93)
8 tbs/120ml coconut milk
8fl oz/250ml/1cup stock/broth
1 tbs/15ml sugar
1 tsp/5ml salt
1 tbs/15ml lemon juice
4 tbs/60ml crushed roasted peanuts (or peanut butter)
4 tbs/60ml dried breadcrumbs

In a frying pan/skillet, heat the oil until a light haze appears. Add the chopped garlic and fry until golden brown. Add the curry paste, mix well and cook together for a few seconds. Add the coconut milk, mix in well and cook for a few seconds. Add the stock, sugar, salt and lemon juice, and stir to blend. Cook for a minute or two, constantly stirring. Add the ground peanuts and breadcrumbs, stir to blend thoroughly and pour the sauce into a bowl.

CUCUMBER PICKLE

A Jad

4 tbs/60ml rice vinegar
1 tsp/5ml sugar
2 tbs/30ml finely chopped cucumber
2 shallots, finely sliced
1 small carrot, finely chopped
1 small red or green chilli, finely chopped

Mix all the ingredients in a small bowl and serve.

PRAWN WRAPPED IN BEAN CURD SHEET

Heh Guen

2 garlic cloves
2 coriander roots
6oz/120g peeled prawns, coarsely chopped
1oz/30g pork fat, finely chopped
good shaking of ground white pepper
1 egg
4-5 bean curd sheets (p. 37), soaked in cold water for 8-10 minutes until soft
oil for deep frying
Sweet and Sour Plum Sauce:
4fl oz/120ml rice vinegar
4fl oz/120ml sugar
1 tsp/5ml preserved plum, stoned

Pound the garlic with the coriander roots. Thoroughly mix together the chopped prawns, pork fat, garlic and coriander mixture, white pepper and the egg. Divide the mixture into 4-5 portions. Wrap each portion in a softened bean curd sheet, making a 'spring roll' shape about 5-6in/13-15cm long. The bean curd sheets need to be handled carefully, as they tend to tear, but you can 'patch' as necessary. You should finish with about 3 thicknesses of

sheet around the pork mixture; make sure you fold the ends in to enclose the mixture.

Steam the rolls for about 10 minutes: you will find that the bean curd sheet tightens about the mixture. Remove and cool. The rolls can now be set aside for frying later on, or wrapped and stored in the refrigerator for frying the following day. They may also be frozen.

Make the sauce. Boil the vinegar and sugar together to make a thick syrup. Add the plum and break it up in the syrup, stir thoroughly to mix. Cool. To finish, cut each roll into 5-6 rounds or diagonal pieces. Heat the oil in the deep-fryer until a light haze appears, then deep-fry the pieces until golden brown. Remove and drain. Serve with the Sweet and sour plum sauce.

PRAWNS IN BATTER WITH TWO SAUCES (SERVES 2-4)

Gung Chup Bang Tod

12 large prawns, beheaded, shelled and deveined, but with tail shell left on
oil for deep frying
Batter:
5oz/145g/1cup wheat flour
½ tsp/2.5ml salt
1 egg
8fl oz/250ml/1cup water
Sauce 1:
4 tbs/60ml rice vinegar
4 tbs/60ml sugar
¼ tsp/1.25ml salt
1 small red or green chilli, finely chopped
Sauce 2:
3 tbs light soy sauce
5-6 coriander leaves, coarsely chopped

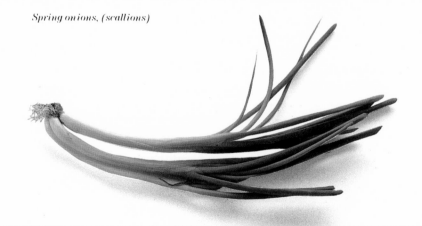

Spring onions, (scallions)

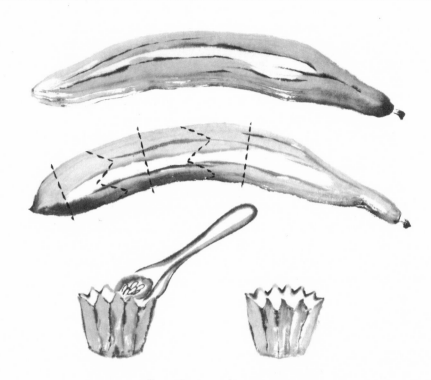

Preparing cucumber cups

Make the batter. In a bowl mix the flour and salt. Break the egg into the mixture, and mix thoroughly. Add the water gradually, whisking the mixture constantly. You should have a thick creamy batter. Heat the oil until a light haze appears. Dip each prawn into the batter, making sure it is thoroughly coated, and drop into the hot oil. Deep-fry until golden brown. Remove with a strainer or slotted spoon and place on serving dish.

Make sauce 1. In a small saucepan, boil the vinegar and sugar together until the sugar dissolves and forms a syrup. Add the salt and stir. Remove from the heat, cool, and add the chopped chilli. Pour into a small bowl. Make sauce 2. Mix the soy sauce with the coriander leaves and pour into a small bowl.

The fried prawns should be dipped by the tail into either sauce. The batter and sauces can also be used for fried strips of vegetable (carrot, celery, beans, courgettes/zuccini etc.)

CUCUMBER STUFFED WITH BEEF
Yam Nua Saweoy

Saweoy is a 'royal' word that means eat. Using courtly language in this context implies something that is small and pretty, and usually delicately carved.

1 cucumber, as long as possible, trimmed at each end and cut into 1in/2.5cm thick slices
6oz/180g lean steak
1 spring onion/scallion, finely chopped
2 tbs/30ml lemon juice
2 tbs/30ml fish sauce
1 small red chilli, finely chopped
1 tsp/5ml sugar
¼ tsp/1.25ml salt
coriander leaves, to garnish

Pre-heat the grill/broiler. Cut the cucumber into sections making alternate straight and zig zag cuts – one cucumber will provide several cups. Using a sharp-edged spoon scoop out the centre of each piece of cucumber.

Grill/broil the steak medium rare. Chop into fine pieces. Mix with the rest of the ingredients. Spoon into the cucumber cups, garnish with coriander leaves.

Wrapping gold bags

PORK TOASTS
Kanom Bang Na Moo

5 slices day-old bread
2 garlic cloves, finely chopped
3 coriander roots, chopped
4oz/120g minced/ground pork
2 eggs
2 tbs/30ml fish sauce
pinch of ground white pepper
1 tbs/15ml milk or cold water
oil for deep frying
coriander leaves, quartered cucumber, finely sliced rings of red chilli etc., to garnish
Serves 4-6

Pre-heat the oven to 120°C/250°F/Gas ½. Trim the crusts off the bread and cut each slice into 4 (or cut into decorative shapes using a pastry cutter). Lay the pieces on a baking sheet/cookie tray and put in the oven for about 10 minutes until they start to crisp. Remove from the oven.

In the meantime, with a pestle and mortar or blender, pound or blend the garlic and coriander roots together. In a bowl combine this mixture with the pork, 1 egg, the fish sauce and the ground white pepper. Mix thoroughly. Put a scant 1 tsp/5ml of the mixture on each piece of toast. Mix the remaining egg with the milk or water, and brush each pork toast with this. Heat the oil and deep-fry, a few at a time, for 2-3 minutes until browned. Drain on paper towels, arrange on a large plate, and garnish with coriander leaves, cucumber, chilli, or a mixture of all pierced with a toothpick. This recipe makes 20 toasts.

This could be served with the *A Jad* sauce (p. 164).

GOLD BAGS
Tung Tong

4oz/120g minced/ground pork
2 water chestnuts, chopped
1 garlic clove, very finely chopped
ground white pepper
12 small wan ton wrappers (about 3 × 3in/7.5 × 7.5cm)
oil for deep frying
Sauce:
4 tbs/60ml sugar
4 tbs/60ml rice vinegar
¼ tsp/1.25ml salt
1 small red chilli, cut into fine rings
1 small green chilli, cut into fine rings

Thoroughly mix the pork, garlic, water chestnut and a sprinkling of pepper. Put 1 tsp/5ml of the mixture in the middle of each wrapper, gather up the corners and squash together to make a small bag. When you have your 12 little bags, heat the oil, and deep-fry until they are crisp and dark gold.

Make the sauce. In a small saucepan, dissolve the sugar in the vinegar and boil rapidly, stirring, for about 10 minutes until you have a pale gold syrup. It will thicken as it cools. Add the salt and the sliced chillies, and stir to mix. To eat, the bags are dipped in the sauce.

THAI FRUIT

More varieties of oriental fruit are now appearing in the West but there is often little guidance available as to how they should be handled. Here are a few tips for the most frequently seen of these new arrivals.

Fresh Lychee While the tinned variety is the most common dessert in oriental restaurants, the fresh fruit is still fairly rare, and absolutely wonderful in comparison to its syrupy cousin. Fresh lychees are served in their brittle shells, which are simply cracked open with the fingers and pulled apart to reveal the opalescent fruit within. There is a stone/pit to discard.

Mango There are details on how these should be peeled and set out on p. 168.

Star Fruit (Carambola) This pretty waxy fruit is cut into horizontal slices to preserve its star shape, and eaten with a fork.

Rambutan This is a sort of hairy lychee. To serve, cut it around the middle, remove the top and offer the fruit like an egg in a hairy cup. To eat, the bottom part is held in the fingers and the fruit drawn out with the teeth. There is a seed/pit to discard.

Mangosteen This is considered by some as the queen of fruit. It has a hard dark purple exterior, almost like a shell, with four greenish leaves on top. To get to the fruit, cut the shell all the way around horizontally halfway down with a sharp knife, being careful not to cut into the flesh of the fruit (the shell is usually about ¼in/5mm thick). You can then lift off the top of the shell to find the creamy white segments nestling in the lower half. You should present the fruit already cut, with the cap replaced, so that diners merely have to lift this off and fork out the segments inside. The largest segments will have a seed/pit to discard.

Star fruit, (carambola)

THAI DESSERTS/KONG WAN

MANGO WITH STICKY RICE
Khao Niew Mamuang

This is the best-known of all Thai sweets yet it is also the least typical, being neither a 'liquid' syrup nor a 'dry' cake. There are several varieties of mango, but the very sweetest are best served in this way so as to balance their rich taste. This is clearly a combination of flavours that approaches that perfect balance we aspire to, for no matter how often it is served one never seems to tire of it.

8fl oz/250ml/1 cup thick coconut milk
2 tbs/30ml sugar
½ tsp/2.5ml salt
10oz/300g sticky rice (p. 138) cooked, still warm
3 large ripe mangoes
2 tbs/30ml coconut cream
Serves 3

In a bowl, mix the coconut milk, sugar and salt and stir until the sugar has dissolved. Mix in the still warm cooked rice, and set aside for 30 minutes. Peel the mangoes, and slice the two outside 'cheeks' of each fruit as close to the central stone/pit as possible. Discard the stone. Slice each piece of fruit into 4 pieces lengthways. Mound the rice in the centre of a serving dish and arrange the slices of mango around it. Pour the coconut cream over the rice and serve.

LIQUID DESSERTS

BANANAS IN SYRUP
Kruay Chu'am

There are many varieties of Thai banana, each with subtle variations of flavour. The stubby finger-like banana (sometimes called 'lady's fingers' or apple banana) is very sweet and there is no equivalent outside the tropics. The long dessert banana, which is usually available in the West, has been ripened in storage and has a poor flavour by comparison. These 'cooked' dishes are probably the best way to serve them.

4 oz/120g sugar
8fl oz/250ml/1cup water
4 bananas
4fl oz/125ml/½ cup coconut cream (optional)
¼ tsp/1.25ml salt (optional)

In a small saucepan, dissolve the sugar in the water over a low heat. Strain the mixture through muslin into a larger pan.

Peel the bananas and chop into 2in/5cm pieces. Add to the sugar mixture. Bring to the boil, uncovered, then lower the heat and cook gently, sprinkling with a little cold water 2-3 times. Remove any scum that forms. When the bananas are bright and clear, and the sugar syrup forms threads when lifted with a wooden spoon, turn onto a serving plate. Serve hot, either just as it is, or with the optional coconut cream, slightly salted.

BANANAS IN COCONUT MILK
Kruay Bua Chee

6 bananas
12fl oz/375ml/1½cups coconut milk
2 tbs/30ml granulated sugar
½ tsp/2.5ml salt

Peel the bananas and chop into 2in/5cm segments.

In a saucepan, heat the coconut milk with the sugar and salt, and cook gently until the sugar dissolves. Add the banana pieces and cook gently for 5 minutes.

Divide the mixture into 6-8 small bowls and serve warm.

ORANGES IN SYRUP
Som Loy Geow

This is a hot weather dessert, and you can serve it over ice-cubes to make it really cold.

4 oranges
8oz/225g sugar
12fl oz/375ml/1½cups water
1tsp/5ml rosewater

Peel and segment the oranges, ensuring that no pips/pits, pith or skin remain. Put the segments in a glass dish and set aside.

While the pudding is baking, heat the oil and fry the sliced shallots until dark golden brown; drain on paper towels and set aside.

About 10 minutes before you take the pudding from the oven, preheat the grill/broiler. When it is cooked, put the pudding under the grill/broiler to crisp the top – about 5 minutes. Leave to cool. Sprinkle the fried shallots over the top, cut into small squares (1-1½in/2.5-4cm) and serve.

JACKFRUIT SEEDS
Met Kanoon

These sweetmeats resemble the seeds/pits of the jackfruit, which are like large kidney beans. They are the nearest the amateur can get to making Look Choob.

8oz/230g split moong beans (available from oriental and Indian stores)
6oz/180g desiccated coconut
2 egg yolks, beaten
8oz/240g sugar
12fl oz/375ml/1½ cups water

Rinse the moong beans, place in a small saucepan and cover with 1½in/4cm water. Cook over a medium heat until completely soft – about 30-45 minutes. Drain off any excess water and mash thoroughly. Add the desiccated coconut and mix thoroughly to form a firm paste. Turn the mixture onto a board, and taking pieces about the size of a small walnut, form into small egg shapes.

Make a syrup from the sugar and water and keep it hot. Dip the 'eggs' into the beaten egg yolks and then drop them into the syrup where they should cook briefly. Remove with a small strainer and set them aside to cool. Serve as sweets or candies.

SAGO AND SWEETCORN PUDDING
Saku Khao Pohd

1pt/570ml/2½cups water
2tsp/30ml rosewater
4oz/120g sago or tapioca
¼tsp/1.25ml salt
4oz/120g sugar
6oz/180g sweetcorn kernels, canned or frozen
4oz/120g lotus seeds (available in cans from oriental stores)
4fl oz/125ml/½ cup coconut cream

In a medium saucepan, bring the water to the boil. Add the rosewater, sago or tapioca and salt, stir, and cook until the grains have fully swelled and are cooked through – about 15 minutes. Add the sugar, stir and cook until the sugar is dissolved. Stir in the sweetcorn and then the lotus seeds.

Divide the pudding into 6-8 small bowls, top each one with a spoonful of coconut cream, and serve warm.

TARO CONSERVE
Puak Goan

1 large taro (p. 39), about 2 lbs/1 kg
8oz/230g sugar
8fl oz/250ml/1cup coconut milk

Peel the taro and cut into 1-1½in/2.5-4cm square chunks. Boil or steam them for 15-20 minutes until tender, then drain and mash well.

Dissolve the sugar in the coconut milk over a gentle heat and add it gradually, a few spoonfuls at a time, to the mashed taro. Mix thoroughly. Sieve this mixture into a saucepan and stir over a medium heat until you can form a soft ball with it. (This is to get rid of excess moisture.)

Spread the mixture in a shallow baking tin, about 8in/20cm square, and allow to cool. Cut into small squares and serve with fruit.

Coconuts and bananas

VEGETABLE CARVING

Visitors to my country are often astonished – and sometimes deceived – by the elaborate ways in which the humble carrot or onion can be transformed into delicate flowers. I am not an expert at this art myself, but still endeavour to make a dish as attractive-looking as possible by the addition of a chilli flower or spring onion/scallion tassel.

The following are simple decorative forms which can be achieved quite easily. It is essential, however, to use a small finely-bladed and very sharp knife – a long-bladed craftwork scalpel would do very well.

Spring onion/scallion chrysanthemum Cut the white root end of a large spring onion/scallion to a length of approximately 2in/5cm. Keep the leafy end to make the spring onion tassle. Trim off the roots, but cut off as little of the solid root end as possible. Hold the base firmly in a vertical position and, with a very fine blade, make at least ten vertical parallel cuts from tip to base to within approximately ¼in/5mm of the base, making sure you do not cut right through at the bottom. With the thumb and forefinger gently ease out the resulting 'petals' to start to make a flower form. Drop it head down into a bowl of iced

Carved vegetables: carrot, tomato, red cabbage, cucumber, spring onion

water for a few minutes, where the flower will blossom.

Spring onion/scallion tassel Trim the top green end of a spring onion and cut a piece between 2-3in/5-7.5cm long, including a ½in/1cm of the white base. With a very fine blade, or a needle, and holding the white part of the scallion as a base, shred the green part as finely as possible. Drop into a bowl of iced water. The fine shreds will curl back.

Two spring onion (scallion) flowers

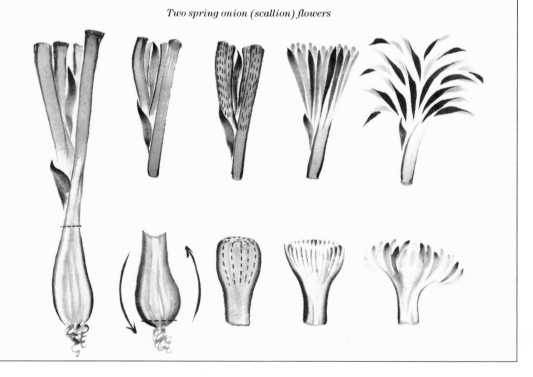

EATING OUT

A PERSONAL CHOICE OF
SOME OF THAILAND'S MANY RESTAURANTS
WITH A SELECTION OF RECIPES

Lakorn, *Thai classical dance photographed in 1911*

id-day and three men in spotless white shirts and dark ties are discussing something serious while dipping into bowls of curried noodles. Their sober dress and way of talking marks them out as government officials from one of the nearby ministries. Beyond the restaurant windows in the wide circus is Democracy Monument, a curious mix of Thai traditional forms and European monumental sculpture in the pre-war heroic style. The friezes represent all aspects of Thai life from the military to peasant farmers and they celebrate the country's first constitution following the abrogation of the absolute monarchy in 1932. The monument stands on an island surrounded by circling traffic at the centre of Rajadamnern Avenue or 'the Royal Way of Walking', one of the city's first major highways, built by King Chulalongkorn to link the old, uncomfortable Grand Palace with his new home, the Vimanmek. This broad boulevard was very popular with his children who used it to satisfy the turn of the century passion for cycling. There are photographs of it in 1908 with a Royal motor procession chugging its length. Such events were apparently very popular which makes me want to weep when I think of the appalling traffic today. After the creation of the constitutional monarchy the avenue was lined with government buildings in Thirties functional style to house the burgeoning bureaucracy. The Vijit restaurant near the monument caters for today's functionaries who occupy these rather forbidding edifices. Decorated in subfusc browns it shows a haughty disdain for fashion, the decor being distinctly secondary to the quality of the food. Its customers may not be rich but they do know what good cooking in the Bangkok style is and here they get it. There are no tourists. Vijit is on no one's itinerary, just characters typical of the capital. A fat Chinese businessman moans and complains to a friend about some permit he has failed to obtain that

Page 178: The Baan Suan restaurant, Chiang Mai

morning all the while placating his distress with large helpings of steamed fish. A young man stares at his fiancée who, with the politeness traditionally expected of young Thai girls, merely nibbles at the food before her no matter how hungry she may really be. If the boyfriend thinks this charming abstinence will last after they are married he need only look at the three women at the table beside him to be disabused. Here are three real Thai civil servants, comfortable of girth and with the major task of the day before them – lunch. They only speak in the interludes when more rice is ladled out. Of course they have good reason, this is a moment to look forward to in a rather dull day and the food is very good indeed and nicely presented without too much fuss, in other words a real city brasserie. Bustling waiters in white shirts and black bow ties complete the picture.

Ever since I opened my own restaurant, eating out has meant something different for me. For one thing, I am always checking up on how other people do it. But more than that, I am always keen to try something new and to work out how I can serve it up myself. All Thai cooks do this and our main source of inspiration remains that marvellous, anonymous legion serving up food on the streets and in the markets of my country. But of course there are also wonderful restaurants like Vijit and I thought it would be useful if on my last visit to Thailand I went round some of the restaurants that I have enjoyed to pass on the atmosphere that makes me appreciate them so much and to make up a selection of recipes based on what these restaurants have to offer. I have not picked these restaurants because they are the 'top ten' centres of gourmet life in South East Asia, but rather because each offers a different experience: some, great food; others, entertainment. The recipes that follow are my own versions of what I have eaten, adapted to suit the ordinary kitchen, a chance to create something a little more spectacular than usual but nevertheless still

Democracy Monument, Bangkok – Vijit restaurant is to the right

within the bounds of the possible. If you do visit Thailand, I hope you will look up some of the places I mention and enjoy them as much as I have.

Across town, near my family house, is Ton Kruang, a restaurant in one of the surviving 'colonial houses' by what was the Sathorn Klong, now an expressway. Here you find an altogether different crowd from Vijit, younger and certainly more fashionable, the sort of people who work in the nearby business district around Silom Road, the banks and finance houses, the airlines and international hotels. These young people are the principal beneficiaries of my country's recent economic boom. They wear the latest fashions, nowadays produced by our own designers, they read magazines that show styles in interior decoration, offer new recipes and suggest interesting places for dining out. The Thai word for what these people are seeking is *Sa-mart* which may sound a little like *Sanuk* but is really only our version of the English word, smart, meaning well-presented or clever. The Sa-mart crowd are always on the lookout for somewhere new to eat and Bangkok boasts many outposts of almost every cuisine: Italian pizzeria, French nouvelle cuisine, German beer huts and of course our own Chinatown with some of the finest Chinese restaurants in Asia. Recently, in the wake of the Japanese economic miracle we have acquired innumerable Sushi bars. But to most Thais all these are just exotic amusements to be tried occasionally.

As far as Thai restaurants are concerned, many come and go with astonishing speed. Because our food is so good at home, restaurants have to offer something more and that means entertainment, usually music or interesting decor. If a new restaurant offers these along will come the Sa-mart crowd for a while but then they will move on to something new and the restaurant will wither and die. Just a few manage to go on being fashionable and my own favourite is Moon Shadow because it both looks pretty yet you can eat well. The restaurant is a long

Fast food Thai style

shrimp paste, coriander root and pepper to a paste. In a small frying pan/skillet, heat the oil, add the paste and fry quickly for a few seconds. Set aside. In a saucepan, heat the stock, add the fried paste and stir thoroughly to mix. Add the fish, bring to the boil and skim if necessary. Add the ginger, fish sauce, sugar and tamarind (or lemon) juice and simmer together gently for 2-3 minutes to allow the fish to cook through thoroughly. Add the spring onion, and stir. Serve in a tureen or individual bowls.

HOT AND SOUR BAMBOO SALAD
Sup Normai

You will find this described as 'asparagus' on some menus. It is actually young bamboo, and can be bought in jars, marinated with yanang leaf. It is normally only available in Thailand, so if you can't find it, use young, or small bamboo shoots; hold the thick end in one hand, and use a fork to shred the bamboo shoots.

3 tbs/45ml stock/broth
2 tbs/30ml fish sauce
1 tbs/15ml lemon juice
½ tsp/5ml sugar
½-1 tsp/2.5-5ml chilli powder
6oz/180g shredded bamboo shoot
1 tbs/15ml ground browned rice (p. 140)
1 small spring onion/scallion, chopped
4-6 coriander leaves

In a saucepan, heat together the stock, fish sauce, lemon juice, sugar and chilli powder. Bring quickly to the boil, add the shredded bamboo shoot and stir thoroughly. Add the browned rice, stir, and turn onto a serving dish. Garnish with the spring onion and coriander leaves.

WING BEAN SALAD
Yam Tua Proo

The success of this dish depends very much on the very fine slicing of the beans. Substitute stringless beans for wing beans if necessary.

8oz/230g wing beans, cut diagonally into fine slices (⅛in/2mm wide)
6oz/180g boiled chicken, without skin, finely shredded
2 tbs/30ml coconut cream
2 tbs/30ml oil
3 garlic cloves, finely chopped
3 shallots, finely sliced
1 tsp/5ml crushed dried red chilli
1½ tbs/22.5ml *nam prik pow* (Tom Yam sauce, p. 80)
2 tbs/30ml ground roasted peanuts
2 tbs/30ml lemon juice
2 tbs/30ml fish sauce
1 tsp/5ml sugar
2 tbs/30ml stock/broth

Boil a pan of water. Put the beans in a wire sieve, dip into the water for a few seconds to

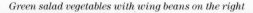

Green salad vegetables with wing beans on the right

blanch and set aside. Have the shredded chicken ready and set aside. Gently heat the coconut cream in a small pan until it thickens slightly, stirring from time to time. In a small frying pan/skillet, heat the oil, add the garlic and fry until golden brown. Remove with a slotted spoon and set aside. Add the shallot to the oil and fry until golden brown and crisp. Remove and set aside. Next briefly fry the crushed dried chilli, remove and set aside. In a bowl, mix the *Nam prik pow* with the ground peanuts, lemon juice, fish sauce, sugar and stock. Add the fried garlic, shallots and dried chilli. Mix thoroughly. Add the shredded chicken and mix; finally add the beans and mix in gently. All the ingredients should be thoroughly blended. Turn onto a serving dish and spoon the coconut cream over the top.

PAK BUNG IN BLACK BEAN SAUCE
Pad Pak Bung Fidang

In Thailand, the plant used in this recipe is called *Pak Bung* but you would find it in Chinese stores as *Kang Kung*. Its English/American name is the rather unattractive Swamp Cabbage, and it is also sometimes known as Water Convolvulus. If you can't find it under any of these names, spinach may be substituted.

This dish takes less than 1 minute to cook!

2 tbs/30ml oil
1 small garlic clove, finely chopped
2 small chillies, red or green, finely chopped
4oz/120g *Pak Bung*
1 tsp/5ml yellow or black bean sauce
1 tbs/15ml oyster sauce
1 tbs/15ml fish sauce
4 tbs/60ml stock/broth or water
½ tsp/2.5ml sugar

Heat the oil, add the garlic and fry until it starts to brown. Add the chillis and fry. Then quickly add the Pak Bung and stir-fry for 3-4 seconds. Add all the other ingredients and quickly stir-fry together. Serve.

YOUNG CHILLI SPICY SAUCE
Nam Prik Num

In the north of Thailand there are young large fresh chillies, coloured pale green, like leaves. This spicy sauce is based on them, but a reasonable substitute could be made using the large fresh green chillies you can buy in the West, though these will be fully matured and dark green. Aside from the chillies, the unique flavour of this Nam Prik comes from the slight burning of the ingredients, a taste found also in North African cooking. This sauce can be served with a variety of cut vegetables – cucumber, carrot, celery, broccoli – and with prawn crackers or pork crackers.

The Aroon Rai restaurant, Chiang Mai

10 garlic cloves
2 shallots, peeled
4 large green chillies
2 medium tomatoes
5 small green aubergines/eggplant or 1 large aubergine/eggplant, peeled
2 tbs/30ml lemon juice
2 tbs/30ml fish sauce
1 tbs/15ml sugar
1 tbs/15ml chopped spring onion/scallion
1 tbs/15ml chopped coriander leaf

Grill/broil the garlic, shallots, chillies and tomatoes for approximately 10 minutes until slightly charred. While these are cooking, put the aubergines in a small pan, cover with water and boil for 5-10 minutes until tender (the cooking time will be slightly less for one larger aubergine). When all the above are ready, cut the tops off the aubergines and skin the tomato. Place these and the other grilled/broiled ingredients into a mortar or food processor, and pound or process this mixture until well blended, but not too fine. Turn into a bowl and add the remaining ingredients. Taste for balance. It should be quite hot and sharp, but if too hot add a little more sugar and lemon juice and perhaps a little more fish sauce.

Large red chillies, beloved of Thais who like their food burning hot

CURRY NOODLE

Gueyteow Keh

2oz/60g dry *Sen Mee* noodles (p. 85), soaked in cold water for 15 minutes to soften, then drained
4oz/120g beef, cubed
1 hard-boiled/cooked egg
3 tbs/90ml oil
1 block prepared fried bean curd (p. 37), finely sliced
1 shallot, finely sliced
1 garlic clove, finely chopped
2 tsp/10ml Red curry paste (p. 37)
4 tbs/60ml coconut milk
1 tsp/5ml curry powder
1 tbs/15ml fish sauce
1 tsp/5ml sugar
1 tbs/15ml ground roasted peanuts
coriander leaves, to garnish
Serves 2

Set the noodles aside, but have ready a pan of hot water in which to warm them. Put the beef in a small pan and cover with water; boil gently for 10-15 minutes. Cut the egg into quarters and set aside.

In a small frying pan/skillet, heat 1 tbs/15ml oil and fry the sliced bean curd until slightly crisp; drain, and set aside. Reheat the oil (add a little more if necessary) and fry the shallot until dark golden brown and crisp. Set aside in the pan. In a wok or frying pan heat 2 tbs/30ml oil, add the garlic and fry for a few seconds until golden brown. Add the curry paste, stir to mix and cook for a few seconds. Add the coconut milk, stir thoroughly to blend and heat through for a few seconds. With a slotted spoon or strainer, remove the beef from its pan and add to the mixture. Stir to make sure each piece is covered with the curry. Add 2 cups of the water in which the beef has boiled (make up the amount with cold water if necessary), the curry powder, fish sauce and sugar. Stir to mix and cook together for about 5 minutes.

Have two serving bowls ready. Bring the pan of hot water to the boil, put the noodles in a sieve or strainer with a handle and dip into the water for 2-3 seconds to warm through. Drain and divide between the serving bowls. Arrange the quartered egg on top of the noodles. Add the peanuts to the beef curry soup, stir, and pour over the noodles. Garnish with the reserved fried bean curd, fried shallots with a little of their oil, and the coriander.

FRIED PRAWN WITH CHILLI AND LIME LEAF

Chu Chee Gung

2 tbs/30ml oil
2 garlic cloves, finely chopped
1 tbs/15ml Red curry paste (p. 37)
2 tbs/30ml stock/broth or water
6-8 large raw prawns, shelled and deveined
2 tbs/30ml fish sauce
1 tbs/15ml sugar
1 tbs/15ml lemon juice
2 lime leaves, finely slivered
1 long red chilli, finely slivered
Serves 2

In a wok or frying pan, heat the oil, add the garlic and fry until golden brown. Add the curry paste, stir to mix, and cook together for a few seconds. Add the stock and mix thoroughly. Add the prawns and turn in the mixture until coated thoroughly. Cook for a few seconds until the prawns become opaque. Stirring quickly after each addition, add the fish sauce, sugar, lemon juice, lime leaves and chilli. Stir thoroughly for 2-3 seconds and serve. This dish should be quite dry.

WHITE RADISH CAKE

Kanom Pad Ga

1 white radish (mooli) (weighing about 2 lbs/1kg)
6oz/180g/1½cups rice flour
2 tbs/30ml wheat flour
2 tbs/30ml water

Trim and peel the radish and cut into small cubes. Using a food processor or blender, mash the radish as fine as possible. This will have to be done in 2-3 batches. When all is finely ground, mix thoroughly with the rice and wheat flours and the water. Turn the mixture into a shallow tin or heatproof dish, about 8in/20cm square, to a depth of about 1in/2.5cm. Heat up your steamer (or use your largest saucepan with an upturned bowl in the bottom on which to rest the tin) and steam the cake for about 30 minutes from the time the steamer is hot. If you are using a thicker dish you will have to steam it for a little longer. When an inserted knife comes out clean, remove from the heat, and allow to cool and dry out completely. It will set more solidly as it cools. Cut the cake into rectangles, about 1 × 2in/2.5 × 5cm.

WHITE RADISH CAKE WITH PRAWN

Kanom Pad Ga Gung

The white radish cake can be served in a number of ways but this is one of my favourites and goes well with *Prik nam som* (p. 86).

3 tbs/45ml oil
1 batch white radish cake
2 garlic cloves, finely chopped
4oz/120g peeled prawns
1 egg
2 tbs/30ml fish sauce
1 tsp/5ml dark soy sauce
½ tsp/2.5ml sugar
shaking of ground white pepper
1oz/30g beansprouts, rinsed and drained
3 spring onions/scallions, cut into 1in/2.5cm slivers
Serves 3-4

In a frying pan/skillet, preferably non-stick, heat half the oil. Add half the radish cake pieces and, stirring and turning constantly, fry until they are browned on all sides. Remove from the pan and set aside. Add the rest of the oil and reheat. Add the garlic and fry until golden brown. Add the prawns and quickly stir-fry for 2-3 seconds. Break in the egg, stir to mix and cook for a few seconds until the egg starts to set. Add the reserved fried radish cake and mix thoroughly. Quickly add the fish sauce, soy sauce, sugar, pepper, beansprouts and spring onions. Mix quickly and thorough-

White radish or mooli

vinegar and sugar together, stirring constantly, until the sugar dissolves and the mixture thickens and starts to brown. Remove from the heat and allow to cool. Add the salt and chilli; stir to mix. Pour into a small bowl.

Steam the pieces of wrapped chicken for about 10 minutes until the leaves are soft. Remove from the steamer. Heat some oil in a deep-fryer and fry the parcels for 5 minutes. Remove and drain. Serve with the sauce.

LITTLE BIRDS
Nok Noy

These chicken 'birds' are a very simple dish, but success depends on your skill with a knife.

6 chicken wings
3 garlic cloves
4 coriander roots
2 tbs/30ml fish sauce
grinding of black pepper
3 tbs/45ml flour
oil for deep frying
Sauce:
8 tbs/120ml rice vinegar
3 tbs/45ml sugar
¼ tsp/1.25ml salt
1 small garlic clove, finely chopped
1 red chilli, finely chopped

From each wing, cut away the wing tip and the first joint (these could be used to make stock). You are now left with the largest, middle, joint. Remove the skin. With a sharp knife, cut between the two parallel bones and separate them at one end. Pull them gently away from each other making sure you don't break the remaining joint. Carefully cut away the meat from the larger bone leaving a small triangle of meat at the tip and fold back over the second bone. The meat will form the body of the 'bird' and the bared bone the neck and head. Gently pierce the meat with a fork. Set aside.

Using a pestle and mortar or blender, pound or blend the garlic with the coriander roots. Turn the mixture into a large bowl, add the fish sauce and black pepper and mix. Add the chicken 'birds' and thoroughly coat them with the mixture. Allow to stand for at least half an hour. Heat the oil in the deep-fryer. Dust the 'birds' in the flour making sure the entire surface of the meat is covered. Fry the 'birds' at medium heat until they are well-browned. Remove from the oil and drain.

Make the sauce. In a small pan, boil together the vinegar and sugar, stirring constantly, until the sugar is dissolved and the mixture starts to thicken. Add the salt, stir, remove from the heat and allow to cool. Add the chopped garlic and chilli, and stir to mix.

Serve in a small bowl to dip the chicken.

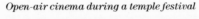

Open-air cinema during a temple festival

The author at a market restaurant near the Old Gate, Chiang Mai

FRIED BEEF WITH CRISPY BASIL
Nua Tod Krapow Krob

Deep-frying the fresh sweet basil leaves gives them a beautiful glossy-green colour and adds an interesting texture to this dish.

2 garlic cloves, pounded
3 coriander roots
2 tbs/30ml fish sauce
1 tbs/15ml light soy sauce
1 tsp/5ml sugar
shaking of ground white pepper
6oz/180g lean beef, cut into thin strips
30 sweet basil leaves (without any stalk)
oil for deep frying

Pound the garlic with the coriander, then combine with the fish sauce, soy sauce, sugar and white pepper. Add the beef, stir to ensure that each piece of meat is coated with the mixture, and marinate for at least half an hour.

Heat the oil and deep-fry the meat until slightly crisp at the edges but not too dry. Remove from the oil with a strainer or slotted spoon and turn onto a serving dish. Add the basil leaves to the oil and fry for a few seconds. Remove with a strainer, drain quickly, sprinkle over the beef and serve.

MIXED MEAT AND VEGETABLE CURRY WITH CLEAR NOODLE
Gaeng Ho

Mixed meat and vegetable curry with clear noodle.

8 tbs/125ml/½cup coconut cream
2 tbs/30ml oil
2 garlic cloves, finely chopped
1 tbs/15ml Red curry paste (p. 37)
1 tsp/5ml ground turmeric
3oz/90g boneless chicken, finely sliced
3oz/90g lean pork, finely sliced
2oz/60g dry *Wun Sen* noodles (p. 86), soaked in cold water for 10 minutes to soften (about 4 oz/120g wet weight)
6 tbs/90ml stock/broth or water
2 lime leaves, finely sliced
2 tbs/30ml fish sauce
½ tsp/2.5ml sugar
4-5oz/120-150g mixed prepared vegetables (eg. slivered bamboo shoot, quartered small green aubergines/eggplant, coarsely chopped green/snap beans)
3 long red chillies, finely slivered

In a small pan, warm the coconut cream and reserve. In a wok or frying pan/skillet, heat the oil, add the garlic and fry until golden brown. Add the curry paste and turmeric, stir to mix, and fry together for a few seconds. Add the coconut cream, stir and cook for a few seconds until the mixture starts to thicken and bubble. Add the chicken and pork, stir thoroughly, and cook for a minute or so until you are sure they are cooked through. Add quickly the remaining ingredients, stirring for a second after each addition. Once the chillies have been added, using 2 wooden spoons or similar implements, toss the meats, noodles and vegetables together thoroughly until all are just cooked through. Turn onto a serving dish.

JUNGLE CURRY
Gaeng Pah Moo

This is a very hot dish that can be made with almost any fresh vegetable that is readily available. The distinctive flavour of Krachai (p. 38) is essential to the authenticity of the dish; but if it is unavailable to you, you can still achieve a very tasty curry.

2 tbs/30ml oil
1 garlic clove, finely chopped
1 tbs/15ml Gaeng Pah curry paste (see above right) or Red curry paste (p. 37)
6oz/180g lean pork, finely sliced
approx. 8fl oz/250ml/1cup water
2 tbs/30ml fish sauce
½ tsp/2.5ml sugar
10 slivers of Krachai (p. 38), if using dried, soak in water for 10-15 minutes to soften
4oz/120g prepared vegetables (eg. 6 thin green/ snap beans, trimmed and cut into 1in/2.5cm pieces, 1 small carrot, slivered, 2 small green aubergines/eggplant, quartered)
12-15 holy basil leaves
2 whole green fresh peppercorns, or 15 dried black peppercorns
1 lime leaf, finely chopped
Serves 2

In a wok or frying pan, heat the oil, add the garlic and fry until golden brown. Add the curry paste, stir to mix and fry together for 5-10 seconds. Add the meat, stir to mix and cook for a further 10 seconds, continuing to stir. Add 2 tbs/30ml water, the fish sauce, sugar and the krachai. Stir to mix and cook for a few seconds. Add the vegetables and the

remaining water and stir for a few seconds. Add the basil leaves, peppercorns and chopped lime leaf. Stir for a few seconds (the vegetables should retain their crispness). Turn into a bowl and serve.

GAENG PAH CURRY PASTE

8 dried long red chillies, seeded and chopped
4 shallots, chopped
2 garlic cloves, chopped
1 tbs/15ml shrimp paste
1 tsp/5ml finely chopped galangal
1 tbs/15ml chopped lemon grass
1 coriander root, finely chopped
1 tsp/5ml salt
1 tbs/15ml finely chopped krachai

With mortar and pestle or blender, pound or blend all the ingredients together to form a smooth paste.

Nightlife, Patpong Road, Bangkok

RECOMMENDED RESTAURANTS

VIJIT

*Democracy Monument,
Rajadamnern Avenue, Bangkok
Telephone 281 6472*

A more typically Bangkok restaurant of the old school would be hard to find. The antithesis of 'smart' or fashionable decor, the bland interior is the correct setting for a place that provides unpretentious good cooking for the civil servants and other nearby office workers.

TON KRUANG

*120 Sathorn Road, Bangkok
Telephone 234 9663*

One of the few 'colonial-style' two-storey wooden houses that have survived the transformation of a once-quiet residential suburb nestling beside a klong, into the city's business centre. A favourite lunch spot for the young and affluent who work in the nearby banks and company headquarters and who expect good food served quickly.

MOON SHADOW

*145 Gaysorn Road, Bangkok
Telephone 253 7553*

Elegant wooden long-house hung about with antique lamps and other bric-a-brac. Last time I ate at Moon Shadow there was a monsoon downpour which gave me the impression I was eating in a house in the rain-forest; for a moment the city seemed a long way away.

D'JIT POCHANA

*1082 Paholyotin Road, Bangkok 9
Telephone 279 5000
60 Sukhumvit Soi 20, Bangkok 11
Telephone 258 1578
23/368-380 Paholyotin Road, Donmuang
(near Airport)
Telephone 531 2716*

Thailand's best known and most successful chain of restaurants. Despite the fact that these are food businesses their standards have remained consistently high. You go to D'Jit Pochana because you know exactly what you will get – no risks with the food and a pleasant if unexciting decor. They are the sort of useful restaurants every crowded city needs; and with a branch near to the airport, a boon for the delayed traveller.

Shopping for a meal in the Seafood Market restaurant, Bangkok

SEAFOOD MARKET

*388 Sukhumvit Road, Bangkok
Telephone 258 0218*

Slightly crazy atmosphere. A cross between a fish warehouse and a cash-and-carry, luridly over-lit and always crowded because it is so bizarre.

TUMNAK THAI

*Ruchadapisek Road, Bangkok
Telephone 276 1810*

Biggest restaurant in the world! A village of Thai houses offering food from every region of the country. I like to try the North East for a non-Bangkok experience. The waiters on roller-skates add a dash of madness.

BUA

*Thanom Liab Menam, Bangkok
Telephone 294 2770*

About the best way to spend a last evening in Bangkok. The main restaurant is another of the vast eateries like Tumnak Thai but it is the two-storey boat that offers the best entertainment – a trip on the river as you finish your meal.

INDEX

PHOTOGRAPHIC ACKNOWLEDGEMENTS

Location photographs unless listed here
are by Michael Freeman
Recipe photographs are by Clive Streeter
Line illustrations are by Jane Evans
(Virgil Pomfret Agency)

The remaining photographs are reproduced by
kind permission of the following:

BBC Hulton Picture Library: p17 (King Mongkut 1868),
p19 (Suburban letter box 1911), p46 (House on a klong),
p102 (Prince Chula 1952), p150 (Ananda Mahidol, King of Siam 1925-1946)

Mary Evans Picture Library: pp28, 66

The Mansell Collection: p18

Photobank: p52 (The Ploughing Ceremony),
p65 (Early XIX Century Thai lacquer design),
p126 (King Rama VII enters Chiang Mai),
p188 (A Remekein show with foodstalls in the foreground
in the time of King Rama V)